FATHER CHRISTMAS

A TRUE STORY

ROWDY HERRINGTON

STORY MERCHANT BOOKS
LOS ANGELES
2019

STORY MERCHANT BOOKS

ISBN: 978-1-970157-16-1
Story Merchant Books
400 S. Burnside Avenue #11B
Los Angeles, CA 90036

http://www.storymerchantbooks.com

Cover & interior formatting by IndieDesignz.com
Illustrations by Danny Donohue

MORE PRAISE FOR
FATHER CHRISTMAS

When Annie O'Neill comes face to face with Father Christmas for the first time it will touch the heart of every reader. This book is a holiday gem.

—Rafaella De Laurentiis

Reading the delightful, touching Father Christmas I could almost smell the baked ham in the oven mixing with the fragrance of Balsam fir and apple cider. It left me with a warm smile and a renewed spirit. It will you, too.

—Michael A. Simpson, president, Informant Media;
author of *Sons of My Fathers*

I'm old enough that I thought I had read, sung, or watched every Christmas story multiple times. Rarely is there anything to do with Christmas that is new or original. Then, along comes Rowdy Herrington who tells with love the story of his mother, a coal miner's daughter, and her coming of age on Christmas Eve when she learned that the true meaning of Christmas is not what is under the tree but what is in the heart. It's a story that should be read every Christmas. I don't know Rowdy, but I say to you, "Well done!" And have a Merry Christmas!

—Larry D. Thompson, author of the
Jack Bryant legal thrillers,
starting with *Dead Peasants*

An instant Christmas classic, with a moving message about the power of love and faith.

—Dennis Palumbo, psychotherapist and
author of the Daniel Rinaldi mysteries

Rowdy Herrington's Father Christmas *is a beautifully written Christmas remembrance that touched me very deeply. Annie's story is luminous, an instant classic.* –Greg Taylor, author and screenwriter, *Prancer, Killer Pizza, Jumanji*

Herrington is a born storyteller. His skills are in full display here as he reminds us all, in the tradition of O'Henry, Dickens, and the Grimms, how the Christmas season can restore our faith in each other.

—John Harrison, writer/director Frank Herbert's *Dune*

The smile came to my face even before I finished reading "Morning," the first part of Father Christmas. Rowdy Herrington's novella is a rare gem, the story of a working-class Christmas, set in Brilliant, Ohio, coal-mining country, across the Ohio River from West Virginia, due West of Pittsburgh, in the middle of the Great Depression. Never saccharine, this holiday story toes a fine line between nostalgia and realism, offering fresh perspectives about grace and joy emerging in a family and community that persist despite the material conditions with which they are confronted. This Christmas story is filled with diversity, authenticity, and heart.

—Thaine Stearns, Dean of English, Sonoma State University

If you have ever wondered what the true meaning of Christmas is, Rowdy Herrington's new novel reveals that truth with an authenticity of time and place and character that is rare, indeed. As you journey into the Depression-era coal-mining town of Brilliant, Ohio, you will discover again why Father Christmas binds us together and brings joy to all who accept the gifts he brings. –Kim Dawson, producer, *Teenage Mutant Ninja Turtles I,II,III*

This beautiful family story makes me believe in Santa Claus.

—Norman Stephens, former head Warner Television,
Village Roadshow

"Innocence abounds in this warm-hearted early 20ᵗʰ Century coal miner daughter's tale. Her wonder at the magic of Christmas reminds us that the most precious things don't arrive in the most expensive gift-wrappings. As she learns who really unloads Santa's sleigh, Annie realizes the truest form of love is found among those closest to us. Rowdy Harrington's tender family story will make you cheer and leave no doubt that Santa really lives."

—James Michael Pratt, *The Lost Valentine*,
a Hallmark Hall of Fame movie and bestselling novel.

A magical, lump-in-your-throat holiday read for the entire family. If you're looking for an antidote to today's commercialization of Christmas, you've found it in this sweet, beautifully told and illustrated story. I can't wait to share it with my granddaughters!" On a personal note, right from its beginning, I was more than a little touched. My father grew up in Rock Springs, Wyoming, in a family of 9 children. His father was a carpenter who struggled to put food on the table. They heated their house with coal the boys in the family (five of them--all of whom ultimately became successful civil engineers) found in abandoned mines. Rowdy's Amos reminds me of both my father and grandfather. It's such a sweet book and story.

—April Christofferson, author of *Grizzly Justice, Buffalo Medicine*

Rowdy Herrington's book is absolutely brilliant, a genuine literary work of art—so many Christmas stories are written & produced every year, with few of them worthy of becoming classics, but "Father Christmas" is definitely a classic, heartfelt in every way. It's Charles Dickens in the 1930's, in the coalfields of Eastern Ohio with the O'Neill family, every nuance so authentic I felt as if I was living it. And I was as worried about every member of that family as they must've been, honestly grateful for the happy ending.

—Parker T. Mattson, author and screenwriter

"I sit here as I finish reading Father Christmas *with tears in my eyes. They are tears of happiness that were brought back to me with this brave family's story. Growing up in what some called a patch town, known only by numbers I can tell you that the author has nailed it right on the head telling it how it was to live in a time when miners went into the black caves to make their living. They were difficult times as the story expresses but families shared their love for one another in many ways and appreciated the smaller things in life. Because of those times when a family had to work together their relationships with parents, brothers and sisters as shown in this well written story, last their lifetime."*

–Patricia Durst Shaffer, founder and retired curator , Windber Area Museum, Winder, PA

For my Mother,
whose story this is.

MORNING

The smile came to her face even before she opened her eyes. The upstairs room was gray in the half-light of dawn as she slid carefully out from under the covers and crawled down the middle of the big bed between her sleeping sisters. Across the room in the little bed, two younger sisters were cuddled together like kittens. She hurried to get dressed. The room was cold and the window was frosted over, but she could see the first hint of the sun coming up over the hills east of the river. Her fingers struggled with the buttons of her sweater, not from the cold but from sheer excitement.

Out in the hall, she tiptoed barefoot over the cold, cracked linoleum past her mother and father's room and at the last moment peeked in. Mama's side of the bed was empty. She'd be down in the basement kitchen already, firing the coal stove. There was baking to be done today, lots of baking. Her father was sleeping on his back, a big lump under the green wool blanket and Grandma's quilt. Air whistled softly out of his nose like wind down a tunnel.

The thickly built man groaned in his sleep and his hand slid out from under the covers as he turned on his side. The girl saw that his index finger was bandaged and the back of his hand was badly bruised. The skin was discolored in a swirl of purple and yellow and his whole hand looked swollen.

His eyes opened suddenly, as if he sensed someone was watching him, and she froze as he blinked at her. Her cheeks flushed in embarrassment.

"Mornin' Daddy," she whispered. A shiver ran down her spine and she hurried to the steps. He grimaced as he flexed his bruised hand and slid it into the coolness under the pillow. His eyes closed again.

Annie O'Neill went down the plank stairs quietly to the living room. She could see her older brother Loyal was still asleep in the day bed in the small dining room. Their dog Pepper lay at the bottom of the bed. His tail thumped the covers when he saw Annie but he didn't give up his spot. Annie hurried to the steep stairs and went down to the basement kitchen.

The low ceilinged room was dominated by a large wooden table with home-made benches on each side and a white china closet that contained the "good" dishes. Annie's mother was at the sink drawing the cold water from a single spigot into a large pot. Mary O'Neill was a big woman with a soft, pleasant face and deep lines around her eyes. She shut the water off and carried the full pot to the coal stove as Annie came down the stairs.

"You're up early," Mary said. She put the pot on the hot iron stove top and opened the oven door to let some heat into the kitchen.

"I thought-cha might need some help. With all there needs doin' today. Reddin' up... Bakin'." Annie smiled broadly. She was practically glowing.

Mary brushed her hair off her forehead and felt a smile come to her own lips. Even when you're tired, enthusiasm is contagious. She held out her arms and Annie ran to her and pressed her face into her mother's apron.

"It's Christmas Eve," Annie said.

"It sure is."

And so the chores began. Annie helped her mother make oatmeal and set the pine table with bowls and spoons. She woke up her sisters and helped the little ones dress. When she came back down with the baby, Loy was just hurrying in from the outhouse. All the O'Neill sisters bundled up and waited their turn, lined up on the split log bench by the door like little dolls on a shelf. They went out into the frigid air in pairs, oldest with youngest, and no one dallied.

By the time they had all visited the privy, Loy was already at the table eating. There was brown sugar for the oatmeal today and he finished his bowl before all his sisters were served. Then he was up like a shot, grabbing his coat from the hook by the kitchen door.

"Where ya think you're goin', buster?" Mary asked.

"Sled ridin' with Alden."

"There's things I need help with."

Loy's face twisted in pain. "Aw, Ma... It's Christmas Eve."

"Exactly," Mary said.

"But Dad said I could... I promised Alden... Please."

Mary sighed and looked up at the electric clock over the sink. "I want ya back here by eleven," she said.

Loy opened the door and ran out into the alley like his feet were on fire. Pepper darted through behind him just before the door slammed shut.

Mary winced at the bang. "I swear to heaven one a these days he's gonna cut that poor dog's tail right off."

Mary looked around the table at her daughters. They were all frowning at her. Maureen spoke up first.

"Mama, how comes he gets ta go sled ridin'?"

Lydia paused as she fed the baby a spoonful of oatmeal. At fourteen, she was the oldest of the six O'Neill girls. " 'Cause he's a boy. An by all accounts they're pretty much useless 'til they're grown."

No one at the table could argue with that logic.

"I guess you're becoming quite the expert on boys," Mary said. "I'm not surprised either, the way you been studyin' 'em night an day." Lydia blushed as her sisters giggled.

"I have not been."

"No? Not even John Travis?"

The girls went instantly dumb and turned to look at their sister. Lydia was speechless too. How did her mother know about her affection for John Travis? She sat there mortified until, to her great surprise, her mother turned back from the stove and smiled warmly.

Mary took up a matter of fact tone again. "They're good people, the Travises."

Lydia managed to nod. She looked over at Annie to confirm what she'd just heard, and yep, Annie heard it too. A big smile broke across Lydia's pretty face. It made Annie smile too, and all the more certain that this was going to be a great Christmas.

Mary picked up the heavy black work boots that had been set next to the stove to dry. She could tell by the feel that they needed to be oiled again. They were still damp so she opened the oven, put the brogues on a pan and set them inside, leaving the oven door open halfway. She looked at the dungarees caked black with coal dust and hanging behind the stove. This afternoon her husband would put them back on and head to the mine. She would wash them on Monday, but they would be just as dirty and black by Tuesday morning.

The sound of heavy footsteps on the stairs made everyone turn. When Amos O'Neill came down into the kitchen, all six of his girls were staring at him. It was a rare sight to see their daddy at breakfast. For the past two years, Amos was nearly a stranger to his own children. He worked six days a week in the mine, second trick, leaving in the afternoon and not coming home until the wee hours of the morning. Usually, the whole brood would have eaten breakfast and gone off to school before he arose, and they would be fast asleep when he finally returned home. So it was on Sundays that the children got to see their father. Sundays, and if they were lucky and the coal bosses relented, a holiday like Christmas.

Amos was barrel-chested, with powerful arms and shoulders and thick legs. He was a quiet man, and not a demonstrative one. He had heavy eyebrows and a thick mustache. The formidable combination made him seem stern even when he wasn't. There was a chorus of "good mornings" from the girls. Amos just nodded.

"What are you doin' up?" Mary asked.

"Couldn't sleep."

"Your hand?"

"I think it's bleedin' again."

"Lem-me see."

Amos came to his chair and sat heavily. Mary took his hand and carefully unwrapped the soggy bandage. Lydia moved closer and peered down. "What happened, Daddy?"

"Slate fall."

When the bandage was off and the wound was revealed, all the girls stared. Isabelle covered her eyes and swooned.

Mary looked over at her girls. Isabelle was pale as paper. "Why don't yins all go upstairs. Annie, give 'em their coats an let 'em go out to play for a while. Maureen, I want ya to dust the livin' room." She turned to Annie. "There's a bucket a water warmin' by the stove. You can worsh the front windows for me."

"Yes, Mama."

Maureen helped Annie herd the girls up the stairs. Annie got the vinegar from the shelf and poured some into the galvanized bucket. She carried it in both hands as not to spill it and climbed the steps one at a time.

"Lem-me see." Mary sat down next to Amos. Amos held out his hand and Mary wiped the blood away with a wet rag. His finger was spilt open in a wide gash.

"Oh Amos, it's bad."

"It's a long way from my heart. Wrap it back up."

"Lydia, get my sewin' basket."

"Oh, for the love a Pete. It don't need sewed."

"Hush."

Amos sighed and looked up at the ceiling. Lydia got the basket down from the top of the china closet and put it on the table in front of her mother.

"Make your father a cup a tea, dear."

"I want coffee."

"The coffee's all. I haf-ta send Loy to the store."

Mary put her fingers in the island of his palm and her thumb on the back of his hand, squeezing softly over the bones and swollen knuckle up to the split finger. Amos winced in pain.

Mary looked worried. "I think it's broke."

"Nah. It's just stoved good."

Mary sighed, opened the sewing basket and as Amos watched, took out her thickest needle and the white thread.

"You gonna use that big one?"

"I'm gonna need it to get through those calluses."

Amos just shook his head. The baby started to cry.

Out on the front porch, Annie brushed her dark hair back just like her mother would and dipped a rag into the steaming solution of vinegar and water. She twisted the rag tight, wringing it out, then set to work on the front windows. It was cold out and the wind was blowing up from the river, but the warm rag felt good in her hands. She stepped around the freshly cut blue spruce that lay on the planks beneath the window and began to hum *God Rest Ye Merry Gentlemen* as she worked.

The O'Neills lived in half a double block, one side of a two-family dwelling in a long row of Eastern Ohio Coal Company owned houses that lined both sides of the dirt and cinder street from the tipple at the mine entrance all the way up to the ridge. The tipple was the center of above ground operations at the mine and so named for the mechanism inside the huge barn-like structure that tipped the mine cars over to empty them.

All the duplexes were unpainted clapboard two stories, weather beaten to a dull gray and virtually identical. They were built dog cheap and were cold in the winter and hot in the summer. The miners often referred to them as the company barns. Someone from the company with a sense of humor had named the cinder track Victory Drive.

The O'Neills' house was near the top of the road. From their porch Annie could look down on the railroad spur to the mine and across the bend in the Ohio River to the hills of West Virginia. As snow began to fall, Isabelle and Molly stood in the rutted street and tried to catch snowflakes on their tongues.

The front door opened and Maureen came out on the porch winding her scarf around her neck. She leaned against a post and folded her arms. Annie glanced over at her but kept working.

"You can't be done already," Annie said.

Maureen shrugged. "I'm fast."

"Sloppy's the word I'd use. Mama 'specs things to be done right."

"I haf-ta dust that room every day. We're hardly in it enough to make it dirty. Go and look your own self if ya don't believe me."

Annie dunked the rag into the steamy bucket and kept both her hands in the water to warm them. She inhaled deeply and smiled.

"Don't-cha just love the smell a vinegar."

Maureen's mouth puckered and her eyes narrowed. "Are they really gonna let ya stay up?"

Annie wrung out the rag. "Yep." She sounded confident but didn't look Maureen in the eye.

"Howd-ja know they will?"

"I'm eleven."

"Yer ten."

"I'll be eleven in February. 'Sides, Mama said I could stay up this year."

"She said maybe."

Annie stopped her work and looked at Maureen with an air of authority. "Ya know if they say maybe, they mean yes."

Maureen nodded slowly at this revelation. Annie raised her eyebrows once and went back to work.

"I'm almost ten."

Annie just shrugged.

"I wanna stay up too!"

"Talk to Mama."

Maureen's shoulders slumped and she stomped her foot on the porch, scattering the snow. She looked back to her sister, the picture of envy.

"What-a-ya gonna say to him? How will ya act?"

Annie turned to Maureen and smiled. She'd been rehearsing this for some time. "I'm gonna say…"

A scream made both girls turn. While looking up at snowflakes, Molly had stepped into a pothole and fallen face-first into the cinder street. Her lip was bleeding, and she was wailing. Annie rushed to her and got her to sit up. She hugged her little sister and tried to soothe her.

"It's okay, Mol. Hold still an' lemme see."

The slate dump below the tipple was steaming as Loy and his friend Alden Reese pulled Alden's Red Flyer sled along Aiken's Creek. Pepper followed behind the boys, zigzagging across their tracks to sniff the odd tree and rabbit hole and leave his mark. Loy winced and rubbed his nose as they approached the dump. All year long it steamed and stunk like rotten eggs as the pyrite in the slate, now exposed to air and water, was busy converting itself to sulfuric acid and iron hydroxide. The runoff caused the entire creek bed to turn the orangish color the locals called "yellow boy."

Loy and Alden pulled the sled behind the railroad shanty and gathered the potato sacks that were piled on it. They peeked around the shanty toward the tipple and the foreman's office.

"I don't see nobody," Loy said.

"He's in there."

The boys ducked back behind the shed as a slate wheeler towing a line of twelve mine cars pulled to a stop on the rails at the top of the smoking mountain of debris. One by one the motorman tipped the wooden cars and the slate tumbled out and down the side of the slope. A whistle tooted behind the boys and they turned to watch a steam engine pull away from the tipple hauling full coal cars down to the spur. Great puffs of smoke, white as cotton, flumed out of the locomotive's stack.

"I dunno," Alden said. The red-headed boy looked worried. His freckled cheeks were already rosy from the cold.

"Don't go poultry on me now. Ya said ya wanted to make some moola." Loy looked his friend in the eye. "Heck, even if they catch us they're bound to let us slide."

"Ya think?"

"It's *Christmas*."

"My Dad'll tan me good if we git caught. Yers too."

"Then we won't *git* caught. We'll pick down at the bottom of the clume where it ain't smokin'. It's safer. And they'd never go all that way after us. If they try, we can be over the crik an in them woods twenty-three skidoo."

Alden wasn't convinced. "Then we'll haf-ta haul the sacks all the ways back up here."

"They don't give that money away, bub. What's it gonna be?"

Alden just stood there, uncertain what to do. Loy looked back up at the foreman's office. No one was in sight.

"I'm goin'," Loy said. He rolled up his sacks, tucked them under his arm and started down the slope, slip-slidin' across the wet shale and slate, heading for the bottom of the stinking gray mountain. Pepper, unwilling to follow, began to bark. Loy turned quickly.

"Pepper!" It was a shouted whisper. The dog stopped barking immediately.

"Go home!" Pepper cocked his head as if trying to understand.

"Go home, I said!" The dog stood his ground. When Loy started back up the hill, Pepper lay down on the snow, his head on his paws. His eyes never left Loy. Loy stopped and shook a finger at the dog. "You stay there then. And be quiet."

The dog didn't move, and Loy turned and headed back down into the slate dump. Alden watched him go, then kicked the ground. At that moment, being left behind with the dog seemed worse than getting caught. He took a deep breath and started down the slope to join his friend.

Loy began collecting the small pieces of coal that had made it through the separating machine in the tipple and gotten discarded with the slate. He used his foot to uncover the black, shiny chunks and then deposited them in the potato sack. Alden began to pick too, but kept an eye on the foreman's shack. He wrapped his scarf across his face and pulled it tight over his nose, but the stench of sulfur was so strong it did little to help.

It was slow work, and after a time both boys were stiff from bending over while trying to balance on the slippery incline. Their noses burned and they were both coughing. Alden stopped for a break, sitting on his half-full sack, and got out his Boy Scout canteen. He took a long drink then offered it to Loy. Loy took several swigs then put the cork back in the top.

"Was ya scairt down there?"

Loy looked up. "In the mine?"

Alden nodded. Loy was the only kid Alden knew who had actually been down in the mine. Rats ran rampant through the mine's shafts and were major pests; so bold they often stole the miners' lunches right out of their pails. Loy had been hired over the summer to shoot them with a BB gun.

Loy handed Alden his canteen. "It's darker than a witch's heart, I'll tell ya that. I was plenty scairt at first. But ya get use-ta it. It's a lot cooler down there in the summer. It's almost a relief." Loy wiped his nose on his sleeve. "It's warmer in the winter too, my Dad says. It stays about fifty-eight degrees no matter what the weather's doin' up here." Loy shrugged. "Anyway, it weren't so bad. Everybody was real nice and looked out fer me. And I got a penny a rat."

"How many did-ya git?"

"Thirty-three."

Alden shivered. "I don't think I could go down there."

"Sure ya could. You can do anything ya set your mind to."

"No sir. You'll never catch me minin' coal."

"Oh yeah?" Loy squinted one eye at his friend. "What-a-ya think were doin' here?"

Lydia was by the door putting on her coat when Annie came back down to the kitchen with the empty bucket and her noisy sisters in tow. As the girls scurried to warm themselves by the stove, Molly burst into tears anew and ran to her mother, wailing.

"What happened, child?"

"She fell and cut her lip," Annie replied. "She's fine." Molly stuck out her lip for inspection. Mary examined the small cut and nodded.

"You haf-ta be careful, honey." She kissed Molly's forehead and this was all that was needed to put the child at ease. "Go and play with your sisters." Molly went to join Maureen and Isabelle who were sitting on the floor now next to the stove with an old hatbox full of homemade paper dolls.

Mary walked to the door and wrapped a scarf around Lydia's neck. She took a knitted dinky from the hook. "Tell Mrs. Collins Merry Christmas for me." She pulled the wool cap over her daughter's head.

"I'll do."

"I wish I had some little thing to send along."

"It's all right," Lydia said. "She understands." Lydia paused at the door took a deep breath. "See ya tonight."

For the past four months, Lydia had worked as a mother's helper for the Collins family. Liam and Joyce Collins lived in a big Victorian two-story on Water Street. Mr. Collins was a foreman for the Company and according to Amos, the fairest of the mine bosses. Mrs. Collins was a kind but exacting woman and their ten-year-old son Sean had Down's Syndrome. At first Lydia was afraid of him, but she quickly discovered that he was a sweet boy. He could be a real handful at times, but he was totally devoted to her.

Annie watched as her sister went out the door into the cold. Even though Lydia was grateful for the job, Annie knew she had grown weary working every day after school, Saturdays and holidays. Lydia never complained, however, and gave all that she earned to her mother.

Mary got out her mixing bowl and the box of Mother's Oats. She emptied a large bag of raisins into the bowl.

"Where'd-ja get them?" Annie was delighted.

Mary smiled. "I have my ways."

Annie finished rinsing the bucket and put it under the sink as an argument arose between Maureen and Isabelle.

"No, you can't do that," Maureen said sternly.

"Yes I can!"

"Nope. It's forbidden."

"Why?" Belle whined. She blinked at Maureen through her thick wire-rimmed glasses.

Maureen held up her doll and smiled with the malice only sibling rivalry can muster. "'Cause mine is the queen. And she says so."

"Mama!"

"Hush, both of you. The baby's sleepin' an yer father's layin' down."

Belle wanted to protest, but thought better of it. Maureen continued to stare at her victoriously. Annie came over then and whispered in Belle's ear. It made a smile appear on the little girl's face.

"Really?" Belle said.

Annie nodded.

Now Maureen looked annoyed. "What?"

Belle held up her doll, beaming. "We live in a..." Belle looked to Annie.

Annie whispered the word in her ear again.

"A de-mocker-sea." Belle repeated. "We don't haf-ta listen ta kings or queens."

Maureen folded her arms and her eyes narrowed as she looked at Annie. "That's cheatin'."

Annie just shrugged. "You would know."

AFTERNOON

Annie sat at the pine table watching as her mother stood at the sink proofing the yeast. Mary crumbled the large white cube up into a bowl of warm water with sugar in it, then set it on the table. "Fetch me the flour from the cellar," she said.

Annie got up and went through the canvas curtain to the small, cool room behind the kitchen where her mother kept the vegetables and dry goods. There was an old, copper washtub set down into the clay floor that served as their refrigerator in winter. The temperature stayed so cool there you could even make jello. There was a chicken in the tub, wrapped in white butcher's paper. Tomorrow it would be stuffed with sage dressing and baked with potatoes and carrots for their Christmas dinner. The mere thought of it made Annie's mouth water.

Most of the shelves were bare, but there were still some jars of stewed tomatoes, pickled cucumbers and hot peppers from their summer garden and jars of applesauce and blackberry jam. Annie and Loy had picked twelve quarts of blackberries from the bushes along the river that summer. Annie baked her first pie with them and even Loy admitted it was real tasty.

Annie hauled the ten-pound sack of flour into the kitchen. She knew her mother would make at least eight loaves of bread today. Mary was tightening the clamp on the bucket of her bread maker to the pine tabletop. The stainless steel bucket could hold enough flour for four loaves, and the paddle and hand crank built into the lid made the mixing easy. It was her only kitchen convenience and Mary loved the machine. Amos had purchased it for her out of the Sears and Roebuck catalog after winning seventeen dollars in a heated euchre game at the American Legion Hall in Steubenville.

As Mary measured out flour she glanced up at the clock and shook her head in frustration. It was a quarter to two. "I don't know where that brother a yours is, but when he gets home…" Mary dumped the flour roughly into the bucket.

Amos came down the stairs in his stocking feet. He was dressed in his work shirt and dirty overalls now. He picked up his boots from the stove side and sat on the bench to lace them up, careful not to bump his injured finger.

Amos' lunch pail was sitting on the table, already packed with homemade bread and butter, two hardboiled eggs, and a small jar of baked beans left over from dinner. Mary had also stashed some of the freshly baked oatmeal and raisin cookies at the bottom of the growler. As Annie watched her father, something about his manner put her ill at ease. Her mother sensed it too.

"What's a matter? Your hand hurtin'?"

Amos sighed and shook his head slowly. "I haf-ta work tomorrow."

"On Christmas!" Mary stared at her husband, but he just tied the laces on his boots and didn't look up.

"Amos…"

"They got a quota."

"But my brother's comin' for dinner! An Sophie an the kids!"

"I know."

"It's Christmas! Don't they have any respect, even for the Lord?"

Amos didn't answer.

"Well, ya can jus tell 'em ya took sick."

"I can't do that."

"Why? Why should you be fair to them when they're not fair to you?"

"It waddn't that long ago we was prayin' for work, remember? Now here it is."

"And we're so much better off for it, aren't we?"

"That's enough."

"It's true!"

"I said that's enough."

Mary's cheeks were flushed now and her arms were crossed over her chest. "Couldn't they at least given ya a half holiday?"

"I told ya. They got a quota."

"So do I! I need my family home on Christmas. That's my quota! What ever happened to all that talk about the union? It was just gas, wasn't it?"

Amos finished tying his boots and stood up. He wanted to go now, Annie could tell. She had heard her parents arguing before, but rarely had she been in the room when it was happening. It scared her to see their angry faces and so she kept her eyes down. The yeast in the bowl in front of her was bubbling and foaming over the top.

"It isn't fair. They promised ya Christmas off."

Amos walked to the door and got his coat off the hook. He turned, and leveled his gaze at his wife. "Ya know what a coal mine is, Mary? It's a hole in the ground owned by a liar."

Mary felt her eyes tear up. She turned away then and found Annie looking at her. She wiped her eyes and tried to smile.

"Get yer coat, Annie. I need ya to go to the company store for me."

Annie was surprised. She had never been allowed to go to all that way on her own. Her father was surprised too.

"She's too young to go by herself," Amos said.

"I'll be eleven in February."

Her father froze her with a look.

"She'll be fine," Mary said. "Sides, she's the only one can go. Lydia's working, and ya told Loy he could go sled ridin' with his friends."

"I most certainly did not."

Annie looked down at her shoes. Loy was really in for it now! A loud scream echoed from above. Footsteps clamored down the stairs and the girls ran noisily into the kitchen.

Isabelle rushed to her mother nearly in tears. "I saw a big bug in the living room! It was yuge and black and horrible! It chased me!"

"It's just a water bug, honey." Mary looked over and saw Maureen smiling.

"You can go right back up there and kill it, missy."

Maureen looked annoyed as she went, but paused at the stairs, mischief in her eyes. "I'll catch it live and bring it back down."

"NOOOOOOO!" Isabelle squealed.

"That's enough!" Amos' harsh tone made Isabelle start to cry.

Mary pulled the child close, her wet cheeks against her apron. "Just go up there and kill it, Maureen."

As Maureen went up the steps, Mary turned to the other girls. "Go an get your book and I'll read yins a story while the bread rises." The girls scurried back up the stairs.

Amos was still at the door. He looked exasperated. He buckled his wide leather tool belt on over his coat and got his pit helmet from the shelf. "I haf-ta go," he said.

He paused at the door for a moment, thinking, then walked to the sink and leaned close to his wife. Mary turned her face away.

They had argued just like this on a hot afternoon this past July. Argued about their company store bill, the coal bosses, and their poverty; matters that they couldn't do a worldly thing about. Amos had slammed the door on his way out. Mary had cried. And later that day as she was standing at the sink, where she was at this moment, she heard a dull rumble. The bell on top of the Stewart School, that dreaded alarm, echoed across the hollow announcing the cave in.

The men from the first trick dropped everything and rushed to the pithead and went straight into the mine to dig out their comrades. Mary and the children waited at the bottom of the hill with the other distraught families for thirteen hours before the survivors were brought out. Amos was one of the lucky ones. Mary had run to him then, and held him with all her might, his face bloody and black. Amos hugged her back and in a hoarse voice made her a solemn promise.

"I'll never go to work again without kissing you goodbye."

Amos had kept that promise. He kissed Mary's cheek now, turned back to the door and went out. Mary wiped her eyes again. "Get yer coat, Annie. Hurry now. You can walk as far as the mine with your father."

Annie quickly pulled on her red rubber boots and her mother helped her with her coat.

"Here's the note. I've written down what I need. Hurry along, now."

Annie tucked the note carefully into her mitten as her mother walked her to the door. "Mama?… Is Daddy mad at us?"

"Of course not. He loves us, honey."

Annie nodded, but seemed unconvinced. "Why's he always so grumpy?"

"He's not." Mary sighed and put her hands on Annie's shoulders. "He has a lot on his mind right now, that's all. He wants us to have a good Christmas."

Annie tried to smile. Mary hugged her hard, then opened the door. "Get goin' now. I want you home before dark." Annie went out the door and waved as she hurried down the alley. Mary called after her. "Be careful."

Mary closed the door and walked to the rocking chair by the stove. She settled into it, leaned back, and rocked slowly. Just as her eyes closed there was a loud shriek from upstairs. Mary looked to heaven.

"God, give me strength."

Annie went down the alley behind the company houses. It was crowded with miners now; clean-faced men making their way down to the pithead, and men with faces blackened by coal dust, on their way home after a long shift in the mine. The miners nodded to each other, exchanged greetings of Merry Christmas, or stopped to shake hands and chat.

Annie hurried past the impromptu groups and ran to catch up with her father. Amos was walking at a brisk pace down the hill toward the mine with his injured hand in his coat pocket. When Annie reached his side he looked down at her but continued his pace. She had to hurry to keep up. She wanted to take his hand but it held his lunch pail. Summoning her courage, Annie looked up at her father.

"You want me to carry your growler, Daddy?"

Amos looked down at his little girl and resisted the impulse to answer no. He recognized the look in Annie's eyes. She was afraid. He handed the pail over to her and slowed his pace. When Annie slid her mittened hand into his, he squeezed it gently. Annie looked up at him and smiled. She was so small, he thought, and yet already so much like her mother.

As they made their way down to the mine no words were spoken, but Annie was glowing inside. For the moment it was just the two of them and it made her feel special, warm, and protected. What an adventure this day was going to be!

At the entrance to the mine shaft, a group of about sixty miners were standing around the elevator, lunch pails in hand. It was a diverse group of Italians, Poles, Hungarians, Slovenians, Irish, and Negros. One of the older miners, a grizzly looking toothless Pole named Waukauski, smiled and pointed as Annie and her father came down the cobblestone steps. Annie grew anxious.

"Who's this now?" Waukauski said.

Amos put his hand on Annie's shoulder. "Your replacement."

All the miners laughed. Waukauski spit tobacco juice and his toothless grin got wider.

"Ain't you funny. What's yer name, deary?"

"Annie O'Neill." Her voice was small.

"How many kids you got, Amos?"

"Seven." Amos squinted one eye. "All boys too… 'cept for six." The miners laughed again.

"Tryin' ta start yer own school?" Jack Duff asked. With his eye patch and gold front tooth, Annie thought the big miner looked like a pirate.

"Two more and I can field my own ball team." Amos winked at Annie. She watched her father joking with the men, and glanced around at all the miners' laughing faces. She had always been afraid of this mine. It was a dreaded place. It made her father dirty, tired, and grumpy and her mother wring her hands with worry. It was a place that was somehow cheating them and all the other families on the hill. It was an unforgiving place where a man could be injured or killed without warning and another man would step right in where he had fallen and take up his task. But at this moment her Daddy seemed so… at ease here.

Waukauski leaned down closer to Annie as he worked his tobacco chaw to the opposite cheek. "Tonight's the big night, eh?"

Annie nodded and smiled.

"Have ya been a good girl, Annie?"

"Yes, sir."

"Ya know what happens if yer not good?

"Ya get ashes in your stocking," Annie replied.

"One year I was-sa bad Sanny Claus left me a stockin' full a coal. I had ta make my own ashes."

Jack Duff laughed. "That was last Christmas, right Gummy?"

"Says you."

"He made his own moonshine and had a real wing ding. Slept out on the porch, positively ossified or he'd a froze ta death!"

The potbellied pit boss, Otto Reitze, came out of the foreman's office. The laughter quickly died and Annie saw the mood of the men instantly change. One arm hung limp at Reitzel's left side; his other hand held a clip board.

"Shift's on," Reitzel said.

Annie watched as the miners moved toward the elevator at the pithead. One of the men, a tall and muscular Negro named Nat Poindexter, walked by with six other Negro miners. He smiled at Annie and nodded to Amos. When Annie turned back to her father she saw the sour face of the foreman frowning down at her.

"What's she doin' here, O'Neill?" Reitzel said.

"She's on her way to the store."

"No kids allowed down here."

"Not lately."

Reitzel was about to say something else, but he swallowed it when he saw the look in Amos' eyes. He waved his good arm instead. "Load it up!"

Amos looked down at Annie. "You better get goin'."

Annie nodded and handed over his lunch pail.

"You watch the road now."

"Yes, sir."

There was an awkward moment and Annie felt the foreman's eyes on them. Amos patted her back gently, then turned and headed for the mine elevator. He was the last one on board. One of the men closed the cage and another threw a switch. The elevator jerked and hummed and began its slow descent. Annie watched as her daddy disappeared, down into a hole as black as a skillet. Down, under the very earth she stood on. Down, to a dark and dangerous place where a man's strength was measured by the ton.

Annie turned and came face to face with Reitzel. She clutched her coat around her neck and hurried off. She went down past the tipple and onto the snow-covered gravel road that led to town. There was no one else in sight now and the wind came cold off the river. The bare trees swayed and shook, their empty branches scraping a lonely sky. She wound her scarf tighter around her neck. Her fingers touched her mother's note inside her mitten, and she quickened her step.

By the time Annie reached the county road and turned north toward Brilliant the wind had died down. The surface of the river looked as flat and shiny as a new mirror. She watched a line of coal barges, pushed by a sturdy tugboat, cut a wide scar through the water as they headed upriver for the steel mills in Pittsburgh.

In the stillness, the air seemed warmer and almost suddenly, a heavy snow began to fall. It was like no snow Annie had ever seen. The fluffy white flakes were enormous, as big as feathers. They floated down softly in the still air, swaying side to side like falling pendulums. The air was so thick with them it veiled the entire landscape. Tree and river disappeared. Annie stretched her arms out and tilted her head back, turning slowly in a circle. She felt as if the sky had opened up and she was standing inside a cloud. This must be what heaven looks like, she thought. She could even hear the soft tinkling of bells.

And the bells were slowly getting louder. The sound was coming from behind her and as Annie turned, she could just make out a ghostlike image coming up the road. A rhythmic clip-clop now accompanied the jingle of the bells. Annie drew a sharp breath as a majestic white horse emerged from the brume of snow.

Annie's eyes went as wide as soup plates. The powerful creature looked gigantic to the little girl. He had huge, hairy hooves that reminded her of slippers, and he trotted effortlessly even though he was reined to a large sleigh. The sleigh was painted as Annie imagined Santa's would be, red and green and trimmed in silver and was being driven by a well-dressed middle-aged man. His wife sat beside him, bundled up in a bright red wool shawl. A little girl about Annie's age was alone on the back seat. She wore a plush white fur coat, with a matching hat and muffler. Annie, in her ten years of life, had never seen anything so beautiful.

Annie smiled in wonder as the white horse pranced by, muscles rippling, steam coming from its flared nostrils. She began running along with the sleigh waving happily to the little girl in the back seat. But the girl just stared straight ahead, a blank expression on her face.

Annie ran along as fast and far as she could but the sleigh was slowly leaving her behind. Finally out of breath, she stopped, and in the biggest voice she could manage, shouted, "Merrrry Christmas!"

Loy and Alden stood outside the Esso station across the road from the Clement Bridge. Three sacks of coal were propped up on the sled with a small cardboard sign handwritten in charcoal: **COAL 5¢**. The boys had left the slate dump with five sacks. Loy had picked three and Alden two. They had hauled the sacks into town and gone door to door to try and peddle them with no luck. So they pulled the sled all the way out to the bridge hoping that someone passing by in a car or truck would see them and stop. In the two hours they were there they had only managed to sell one sack each, one to the attendant in the Esso station and one to a passing motorist. It had been over an hour since they'd even seen an automobile. The boys were getting discouraged.

A streetcar came up the tracks clickity-clacking its way north along the river. Loy watched it glide by, the wheel at the top of the trolley pole, sparking along the unshielded wire.

"One a these days we gotta take the electric in to Steubenville and see us a movie," Loy said.

"We ain't even got the car fare."

"I know. But one a these days."

"I wanna see another double feature," Alden said.

"Who don't?" Loy was envious that Alden had seen *Lives of a Bengal Lancer* and *Trails of Adventure* this past summer. Mary had taken Loy and four of his sisters to the Odeon Theatre that summer too. The movie palace was the most majestic place he had ever seen. It was cavernous with huge columns gilded in gold, velvet seats and plush red carpeting. The domed ceiling was painted deep blue and little starlights twinkled in the artificial firmament. They had sat in the balcony and even had popcorn. But the girls had gotten to pick the movie, and they chose Shirley Temple in *The Little Rebel*. Loy loved the movie but told his friends it was just okay. "I wanted to see *Mutiny on the Bounty*," he had said, "but I was outvoted four to one."

Alden stamped his boots on the snow and shook his head. "My feet are froze."

"Mine too. Hey, lookee there."

Loy pointed at a car coming across the bridge and quickly picked up the sign, holding it out for the driver to see. The old Ford slowed down, but only to turn north on the county road toward Steubenville.

"Aw, heck," Loy said as he dropped the sign. "What time ya think it is?"

"Gotta be close to three."

"I was s'posed to be home at eleven."

"Yer in Dutch then."

"And how."

"What-cha wanna do?"

Loy looked up and down the empty road and shook his head. "Go, I guess."

Loy picked up the rope tied to the steering bar of the sled. "I'll pull first." Alden nodded and got behind the sled to push. The boys trudged off through the snow heading south for Brilliant.

The Eastern Ohio Coal Company store was a tall, red-brick building on Main Street, across from the railroad station. Annie walked through the glass double doors relieved to have finally arrived.

The store served as a combination grocery and department store and also held the town post office. It seemed vast to Annie, packed to the ceiling with shelves of food and vegetables, bolts of cloth and muslin as well as factory-made clothes. There was a butcher's shop, a shoe department, and a drug counter, where one could buy all kinds of patent medicines and sickroom needs. Tools and hardware were sold in the basement along with simple furniture, beds, and mattresses.

Annie picked up a basket and walked up the main aisle of the store. It was crowded with shoppers, mostly miners' wives, some of whom had walked seven miles from their patch at the Glenville mine. Annie already had her mitten off and was examining the note her mother had written. "Two quarts of Milk, a pound of coffee, yeast, 2 pounds of beans"... A look of dismay came to Annie's face.

"Eggs?... Oh, no."

When Annie had collected all the other items on the list she walked to the cooler to get two bottles of milk. The eggs were in a big bowl on a shelf next to the cooler. Annie picked the largest ones she could find and put them into a paper sack. She checked the list again just to be sure she hadn't missed anything, and then she got in line at the counter. The basket was already getting heavy for her and the thought of the long walk home toting the groceries began to worry her.

The clerk at the counter was a balding gentleman of fifty. He smiled at Annie as he took the basket from her. He totaled up the items and wrote the number on a pad. He handed the tab to Annie.

"You need to get a credit slip, honey."

"Yes, sir."

Annie turned and looked into the credit office. Whenever she had come here with her mother, this was the part that always made her feel uncomfortable. By going in and asking for credit, they were always made to feel as if they were asking for charity.

A tall blonde woman in a man's overcoat stood in front of the credit desk. The credit secretary, Miss Johnson, was a thin old woman with gray hair pulled into a tight bun. Her face was deeply lined and she wore half glasses on the end of her sharp nose. Miss Johnson was a spinster, and as far as Annie knew, had never said a kind word to anyone. The fact that no one liked her didn't seem to bother the old witch in the least.

Miss Johnson's desk was on a raised platform, two steps above the floor. A balding bookkeeper in a bow tie and sleeveless red sweater worked at another desk in the back of the office. A 1935 calendar hung on the wall behind the old woman. All the days in December up to the twenty-fourth had black X's through them. Miss Johnson stamped the blonde woman's tab and passed it back across the desk. The woman looked relieved.

"Next," Miss Johnson said.

Annie stepped up to the desk.

"What's the name?"

Annie cleared her throat. "O'Neill." She handed over the tab she got from the clerk.

Miss Johnson turned the pages of the big book, her thin finger moving down the left column. The finger stopped and slid across the page. She looked down at the tab then over her glasses at Annie. The look told Annie the old woman knew everything there was to know about the O'Neill family's finances. It made Annie shiver.

A tall man with uneven, closely cropped hair and dirty miner's overalls, strode into the office and right up to the secretary's desk. His voice was loud and his face pinched in anger.

"I wanna see Dunlevy."

"Mr. Dunlevy's gone for the day," Miss Johnson said.

The bookkeeper slid his chair back and turned, sensing trouble.

"My wife come in here taday and wanted ta buy some meat on tick. An' you people told her our due bill was too high an you wouldn't carry us.

The secretary exchanged a quick look with the bookkeeper. "What's the name?"

"Halechko. George Halechko."

The old woman turned the pages of the book and scanned the column. "I'm afraid that's true. You missed two weeks of work, Mr. Halechko."

"I broke my arm. I went back on Monday." Halechko pulled up the sleeve on his coat to reveal a cast on his wrist.

"I'm afraid the rules are the rules."

"An ya make 'em up ta suit yerselves."

Annie saw Miss Johnson's eyes narrow. "I can't help you. You'll need to see Mr. Dunlevy after the holiday."

Halechko slammed his hand down on the desk so hard it made Annie jump. The Clerk from the counter appeared at the door now. The angry miner leaned into the desk making the old woman sit back in her chair. His face was red as a bandana.

"Now you listen ta me. My wife is seven months along an feelin' poorly. She needs some meat. If ya don't give it ta me, I ain't workin' another day in yer stinkin' mine. Ya hear me? I ain't workin' another day an you'll never git the money I owe ya."

Miss Johnson coldly met the miner's gaze. "That would be entirely your choice to make, Mr. Halechko."

Annie thought Mr. Halechko was going to explode. The bookkeeper intervened.

"Margaret... Give the man some credit."

She glared at the bookkeeper, but he stared right back.

"You can answer to Mr. Dunlevy, then."

The bookkeeper turned back to his work.

Miss Johnson scribbled out a credit slip and pushed it across the desk. Mr. Halechko snatched it up and walked out. The old woman stamped

Annie's tab and shoved it across the desk.

Annie could feel her cheeks begin to burn. "Merry Christmas," she said softly. The old woman just stared at her. Annie picked up the tab and walked out the door.

As she made her way back to the counter, Annie walked past shelves stocked with an array of Christmas decorations, bright wrapping paper, toys and games, baseball gloves, bats and balls, and a whole shelf of dolls. A little girl in pigtails was staring longingly at a beautiful handmade dollhouse. It was her friend, Debbie Abbott.

"Annie!"

"Hi, Debbie."

Isn't it beautiful?"

Annie nodded. She opened the roof of the dollhouse and looked inside. Each room was decorated with tiny, intricately made furniture. Annie sighed in admiration.

"Where's your mom?" Debbie asked.

"At home."

"Did Lydia bring ya?"

Annie smiled and shook her head.

"Loy?"

"No. I came by myself."

"Really? I can't even go to the orchard by myself."

"This is nothin'. Tonight I get to stay up."

"You're gonna stay up? You mean until…"

Annie's smile widened. "Until Santa comes."

"Howd-ja get permission?"

"I'm gonna be eleven in February."

Debbie nodded, dumbfounded. "Annie O'Neill, you lucky dog."

Annie was in her glory.

"Do ya think he'll know ya?" her friend asked.

Annie thought this over, then shrugged. "He gets the presents right every year."

Debbie nodded. "Wow. What are ya gonna do when he comes in?"

Annie had her answer ready. "I'm gonna wait by the Christmas tree 'til he's finished his work and had his milk and cookies. Then I'm gonna walk up to him and say, 'Thank you, Santa, for all the wonderful presents you bring us every year.'"

"That's all?"

"I'll probably be lucky to get that in."

Debbie shook her head in envy. "You lucky dog."

"Amen," Annie said.

Debbie's mom, Mrs. Abbott, appeared in the aisle with her groceries. She looked harried. "Let's go," she said.

She took her daughter's hand and started for the doors. Debbie looked back at Annie and waved. As they opened the door, Debbie asked, "Momma, can I stay up an see Santa Claus tonight?"

"No."

They went out the door and it swung shut with a bang.

Annie stepped up to the counter and handed her credit slip to the clerk. He examined it, then smiled and pushed a large paper sack over the counter to Annie.

"It's kinda heavy," he said.

"I can manage."

"Anything else, then?"

She looked up at him and shook her head. The clerk glanced over his shoulder into the credit office, then quickly reached into a jar and took out a small peppermint candy cane. He offered it to Annie. When the little girl didn't take it, the clerk said, "It's all right. " He put his finger to his lips and winked.

Annie took the candy and stashed it into her pocket. She smiled gratefully. "Thank you."

"You be careful with that package now. It wouldn't do to break the eggs."

"Yes, sir. I'll be careful," she said. "Merry Christmas."

"And a Merry Christmas to you."

Jacob Cohen sat in a chair by the front window of his drugstore and looked out on the snow-covered Main Street of Brilliant. His fingers held an open letter and he tapped it gently on his knee. The letter was from his sister in Dresden, Germany. Jacob looked down at the stamp on the envelope, a German swastika, and sighed. He was worried about Hannah, her news was very troubling. This year, Hitler and his Nazi Party had passed a series of decrees called the Nuremberg Race Laws. These new laws excluded Jews from all public office and civil servant positions. They also made it a crime for Jews to marry outside their faith. Jacob lit his pipe and exhaled a blue cloud of smoke. It was time for Hannah and her family to come to America. That he was sure of.

The old man looked out the frosted window and saw Loy and Alden pulling the sled loaded with the sacks of coal through the deep snow. The boys had come by his store earlier trying to sell him a sack, but Jacob had turned the boys away. Now, as he watched them struggle through the rutted street, he shook his head slowly. Jacob put down his pipe, rose, and hurried to the door.

"You! Boys! Viat! Come here, please."

Loy and Alden turned the sled around and dragged it over to the front door of the drugstore. Their faces were red and their limbs stiff from the cold.

"How much for that coal there?"

"A nickel a sack," Loy answered.

"Okay then. I'll take them."

Loy and Alden exchanged a look of astonishment. "Yes, sir!" They answered in unison.

Each boy grabbed a sack and lugged it off the sled. Jacob stepped out into the cold and took the third sack. The boys followed him back into the drugstore.

Alden was struggling with his sack. When he stopped to rest, Loy watched as the pharmacist effortlessly picked it up. Jacob now carried a sack in each hand and Loy was impressed by the old man's strength.

"Come with me." Jacob said. As Loy followed him back into his apartment, Alden stood shivering by the front door radiator.

Loy had never seen the back of the drugstore before. Mr. Cohen's apartment was furnished with fine old-world antiques and a plush Persian carpet. A Tiffany lamp glowed in the living room; its glass shade a swirl of color. Rachel Cohen stood at the stove in the small kitchen and Loy took in the unmistakable aroma of roast beef. Mrs. Cohen shook her head and smiled as she watched her husband toting the coal sacks over to the cellar door. The old man just shrugged.

Loy followed Mr. Cohen down the wooden steps slowly, straining to keep control of his sack. Jacob crossed to the coal bin and tossed the sacks inside. He came back and took the third sack from Loy, and as he tossed it in with the others, Loy could see that the coal bin was completely full. He looked up at Mr. Cohen then and the old man met his gaze.

"Your friend is vaiting."

As they passed back through the apartment, Loy saw a large framed photograph of a young man in a German Army uniform. This was the Cohen's son, David, killed at the battle of the Belleau Wood in France in 1918. Next to the photograph was a silver menorah with nine candles in it. Loy knew that there was a Jewish holiday called Hanukah, but he didn't know what it meant. He made a note to himself to ask Max Rubenstein about it. Max was the only Jewish boy in Loy's class. They had never really talked much, but Loy was sure that Max would know.

Loy followed Mr. Cohen back into the drug store and watched as he went to the cash register and took out three nickels. He handed them to Loy and Loy gave one to Alden. The boys were grinning ear to ear. Loy had three nickels now!

"Can I buy somethin'?" Loy asked.

"Of course," Mr. Cohen said.

Loy walked down the aisle to look over the notions. His eye went immediately to a gold colored jar that contained cold cream. Even the lid was shiny gold. Loy picked it up and unscrewed the lid. The lavender fragrance was heavenly.

Loy looked up at Mr. Cohen. "How much for this?"

"Twenty cents."

Loy's face fell. He started to put the jar back.

"Vait, I'm wrong. That's the one that's on sale. Fifteen cents."

Loy was beaming now. He handed over his three nickels to Mr. Cohen. "It's for my mom."

"I'm sure she vill love it."

As Alden picked out a whole bag of penny candy, Mr. Cohen put the cold cream in a bright red bag, tied it closed with some yarn and handed it back to Loy.

"Thank you, Mr. Cohen."

"You're very velcome, son."

"Merry Christmas." It was out of Loy's mouth before he even realized it. Had he offended Mr. Cohen?

The old man just smiled. "And peace and good vill to men."

The bell tinkled as the boys went out the door into the snowy street. As they walked along the road, Loy shook his head.

"His bin was full."

"What?"

"His coal bin. It was full up. He didn't need our sacks"

"Then why'd he buy 'em?"

"I dunno. Maybe he jus' wanted to help us."

Alden looked puzzled. "But he's a Jew."

Loy thought about this, then shrugged. "Jesus was a Jew."

Alden stopped in his tracks. "He was not!"

"Was too."

"Was not."

"Ask Reverend Siebert if ya don't believe me."

"Really?... That don't seem right."

Loy just shook his head and walked on.

Annie O'Neill trudged through the ankle-deep snow of "the orchard," an open pasture halfway down the hollow from the mine. A row of ancient apple trees grew along one side of the field and legend had it they had been planted by Johnny Appleseed. In summer the boys played baseball here and, in the fall, the scraggy grounds became their gridiron. The face of the field, now the empire of rabbit, mice and mole, was covered in a crusty white beard. Annie had made an error of judgment and had left the road to take the more direct path up the hill and through the orchard. But she hadn't counted on the steepness of the climb, or the snowdrifts. Annie was exhausted.

She brushed the snow off the weathered plank of a seesaw and sat down to rest with the heavy grocery bag in her lap. She looked across at a rusty swing set. The chains were pulled up to the top of the bar and it was dripping with icicles the size of dinosaur teeth. A chime of wrens rose in alarm from the ground around the swings and headed south, then, as if they had changed their minds as one, veered off like a tumbling cloud toward the purple-red crack of light to the west.

The sun was close to setting now and Annie looked up the hill, despondent. She wasn't sure she could make it the final mile, and she battled back her tears. But then in the twilight a single red Christmas light winked on in the window of one of the houses on the hill. It was a glowing beacon that lifted her spirits and with them her legs. Annie rose, took a deep breath and started the long climb home.

Pepper was lying on the back porch of the O'Neill house, an old rubber ball between his paws. He raised his head then barked and hopped to his feet as Annie came up the path and into the alley. Annie smiled at the welcome. She had made it! The exuberant dog bounded off the porch and raced toward Annie and her relief turned quickly to panic.

"No, Pepper, down!"

But it was too late. The dog jumped up on the weary girl to greet her, and she slipped on the icy ground and fell backward. The grocery bag flew out of her hands and landed in the snow. Pepper licked Annie's face until she was able to push him off her.

"Get away, Pepper! Look what-cha made me do!"

Annie scrambled to the grocery bag and picked it up.

"Oh, no!"

The back door of the house opened and Mary stepped out on the porch.

"There you are. I was gettin' worried."

As Annie came up on the porch, her mama took the grocery bag from her and felt the weight of it.

"Oh Lord. You must be exhausted. Hurry inside, the heat's gettin' out."

They entered the busy kitchen and Mary closed the door. Newspapers had been laid in a path around the clean floor.

"Mama, Pepper..."

"Leave him out there. He's being punished."

Annie was immediately surrounded by her sisters. Maureen unwound her scarf as the others helped her off with her coat and boots. Annie was like a puppet. The kitchen smelled delicious and Lydia was taking more freshly baked cookies out of the oven.

As the girls hung up Annie's coat and hat, Mary set the package down on the drainboard and began unpacking it.

"Mama," Annie said.

"What, dear?"

"It was real slippy... and Pepper..."

Mary opened the paper sack of eggs. None were broken! Annie felt a sigh escape her and she sat down at the table, limp as a dishrag.

"Look at-cha, ya poor thing," Mary said. "Lydia, give her a cookie and some hot tea."

Lydia poured tea from the pot brewing by the stove. She brought the tea to Annie along with one of the cookies still warm from the oven. Lydia was wearing a new apple-green lambswool sweater.

"Wow," Annie said. Where-ja get that?"

Lydia was beaming. "A Christmas present from Mrs. Collins."

"It's beautiful, Lydia," Annie said.

"Thank you. Don't-cha love the color?"

Annie nodded.

Molly tugged on Mary's apron. "Can I have a cookie, Mama?"

"No. Ya had yours. It'll spoil your supper."

Molly came over and sat next to Annie on the bench. She put her little elbows on the table and her chin in her hands. She watched Annie eat the cookie, seeming for all the world as if she were starving to death. Annie looked at her little sister's big blue eyes, then over to her mother. Mary had her back turned to the sink. Annie put her finger to her lips and then broke off a piece of the warm cookie. She handed it to Molly… and winked.

Pepper began to bark out on the porch and then the kitchen door opened. The dog bolted in and immediately ran upstairs. Loy quickly closed the door, grateful to be out of the cold.

"Loyal O'Neill."

Loy already knew he was in trouble, but when his mother used both his names his spirits sank. Mary was staring at him hard. Her face was flushed red and she was really mad. It made Loy feel terrible.

"Where've ya been?"

Loy didn't answer. He couldn't tell her.

"Didn't I tell ya to be home at eleven?"

"Yes, ma'am."

"What time is it now?"

Loy looked up at the electric clock. "Quarter ta five."

"You deliberately defied me. I had to send your sister to the company store."

Loy kept his eyes down but stole a glance to Annie.

"I'm sorry," Loy said.

"Sorry's not good enough, buster. Just wait 'til your father gets home. Christmas or no Christmas you're goin' to the woodshed."

"Yes, ma'am."

"Now get outta those wet things before ya catch your death."

Mary turned her back on him and moved to the stove to check on her soup as if she were too disgusted to look at him anymore.

"And stay on the newspapers. I just scrubbed the floor." Lydia added with disdain.

Loy gave her a look for piling on, but knew better than to say anything right now. It had gotten very quiet in the kitchen. All the girls were staring at Loy as he hung his wet coat on a hook and undid his boots. Annie felt badly for him.

"Guess what I saw on the way to the store?" Annie said. This quickly got everyone's attention.

"A horse-drawn sleigh. The horse was yuge and white as snow. They went right up the road nice as you please. The people were all dressed in fur hats and they were having the best time. They…"

There was a knock at the back door. Mary turned from the stove. Loy went to the door and opened it. A tall and rail-thin man with a ragged beard was standing on the back porch. His arms were folded over his overcoat and he wore a knit cap tight around his ears.

"Is yer mudder home, son?"

"Ma."

Mary came to the door and looked out at the strange man. "Yes?"

"I hate to trouble ya, missus. But I was wonderin' if-in a man could find some work here in exchange fer a little food?" The man's smile showed his two front teeth were missing.

"We don't have any work for ya. I'm sorry."

The man nodded solemnly. Mary looked at the man's worn shoes. They were soaked through from the snow. He was shivering and his eyes were sad.

"Thank you, missus." He turned to go.

"What's your name."

"My name? It's Tom Cotton, ma'am."

"I can give you a meal, Mr. Cotton. Why don't-cha come in."

CHRISTMAS EVE

The children sat at the pine table watching Mr. Cotton as Lydia served everyone their barley soup. There was a fresh loaf of bread on the table, and Mary sliced off a big piece for the stranger. She noticed how dirty his hands were.

"Your welcome to use the sink to wash up, Mr. Cotton."

"Thank you, missus. Forgive my poor manners."

The thin man got up and washed his hands and face at the sink and Mary gave him a cloth to dry himself. When she settled into her seat at the table, Mary looked up at her son. "Loyal, I think you should say the grace."

"Yes, ma'am."

Everyone bowed their heads. Loy closed his eyes.

"Heavenly Father," Loy began, "we are grateful for all your blessings and we thank ya, Lord, for this food we are about to eat." Loy opened one eye and peeked at his mom. He added, "And we thank ya for our dear mother who worked so hard to make it."

Mary's eyes popped open and Loy quickly shut his. Buttering me up is NOT going to work, she thought.

"Amen, Annie said.

"Amen," they all said.

Mary nodded and everyone picked up their spoons.

Annie watched Mr. Cotton devour his bread and soup. He ate with relish, making soft moans of pleasure and it was clear to her it had been some time since he had had a meal.

"I 'spect this is the finest soup I ever et, missus. And the bread... is jus dee-vine."

Mary smiled. "Thank you. Lydia, give Mr. Cotton some more soup." Mary sliced another thick piece of bread for him and he nodded gratefully.

When they were finished with their meal, Mary poured the stranger a cup of hot tea and offered him an oatmeal cookie. The stranger was delighted. Lydia got up to put the big boiler on the stove to heat water for the children's baths.

"Where ya from, Mr. Cotton?" Loy asked.

"I was born in Glidden, Wisconsin, son, but it's been a long spell since I seen it. My folks passed on when I was twelve and I been on my own ever since." A whole cookie disappeared into his mouth.

"Are you a tramp?" Maureen asked.

"Maureen!" Mary glared at her daughter. Annie was mortified.

"Well, I 'spect I am. But we call ourselves hobos. I been ridin' the rails for the best part of twenty years now, gittin' work where I can. I been a gandy dancer, shod horses, even tried my hand at apple knockin'.

Loy looked confused. "Apple knockin'?"

"That's farmin', son. I had me a little place in Arkansas, but it turned ta dust and blew away with the wind. I went out west and worked fer a time on that Boulder Dam in Nevada. It was hotter'n the devil's kitchen, let me tell ya. Jus past I was workin' at a coke oven over in Wheelin', but they cheated me so awful I up and quit on 'em. So's I'm looking ta catch me a ride south fer the winter."

"You hop freight trains?"

Mr. Cotton nodded to Loy. "Next rattler that comes on. We call it ridin' the blinds. Them tracks look like Venetian blinds, see. "

Loy was delighted. "You got our own lingo fer things."

The stranger smiled. "Yeah. We sure do. A locomotive's a hog. A coal car's a battlewagon. A caboose is a crummy. Yer engineer, now he's a hoghead, the conductor is a con and the yard boss is a drummer. Ya gotta watch out fer them. They don't take kindly ta free riders."

"Hoghead," Loy repeated with a smile. Annie smiled too.

"Yep. Ya get yer turkey, see and ya wait fer a red ball on the soup line. Ya can jump off at any town ya choose and head fer the Sally Ann fer that angel food. Hot flatcars and pups, a set a headlights and a ice-cold glass a moo juice."

Loy was grinning ear to ear. "Moo juice is milk."

"Yep. A turkey is yer suitcase. A red ball is a fast freight and the soup line, that's what we call the Southern Pacific Railroad."

"What's Sally Ann?" Annie asked.

"The Salvation Army. Ya git yerself a mission meal. That's angel food, deary. Hot pancakes, sausage, and fried eggs."

"A set a headlights," Loy said with a smile.

"Exactly." Mr. Cotton showed his toothless grin.

"When I grow up I wanna ride the rails," Loy said.

The colorful stranger turned serious and shook his head. "I can't say as I recommend it, son. Half the time yer hungry and freezin', the other half yer jus hungry. And it ain't all that romantic sleepin' out in the open with only the moon for cover or on boards harder than a banker's heart."

Mr. Cotton looked over at Mary then back at Loyal. "No, son. A life a ramblin' ain't all it's cracked up ta be. My advice ta you is ta study yer letters. Most all the success in this world is done by educated men. Ya git yerself some good schoolin' so's ya can be one of 'em."

Loyal shared a look with Annie and she nodded.

Mr. Cotton looked up at the electric clock, then stood up. "I 'spose I best shoe-fly. There's a rattler with my name on it a comin' through 'bout seven."

Mary took a half loaf of bread and put it into a paper sack. She offered it to the stranger.

"I can't take that, missus. Ya got lots a mouths ta feed here."

"It's all right," Mary said.

Tom Cotton took the sack and for a long moment just stood there looking down at it. "I wanna thank you people fer yer kindness."

Mary nodded. "Merry Christmas, Mr. Cotton."

"And Merry Christmas ta you." He waved to the children. "Merry Christmas, kids."

A chorus of Merry Christmases echoed back.

Mary walked him to the door. "Mr. Cotton, can I ask you a question?"

"Sure thing."

"You're the fourth man this year to come to my house askin' for… work. But none of my neighbors have had a single one." Mary shook her head. "I was just wonderin'…"

Mr. Cotton nodded and looked away. After a moment he turned back to Mary. "Yer house is marked."

"Marked?"

"To let a travelin' man know there's a kindly soul here."

"How's it marked?"

Mr. Cotton leaned his head to the side and shook it slowly. "I'm sorry. I can't tell ya that." He opened the door and looked back. "But God bless ya, missus. And all a yers."

With that the stranger went out the door into the cold night.

Thirteen hundred feet under the earth, Amos O'Neill was kneeling waist-deep in cold water. He was bailing out a twenty-foot-square room cut into the coal seam that was his workspace for the night. The roof of the room was the height of the seam itself, an average of just forty inches. The seam had begun to leak badly after the last load of coal had been "shot down" by Amos' charge of black pellet powder. The flooding of the room was bad luck, but there was nothing to be done but bail it out and get back to loading. More water than coal was taken out of the mine, more slag than coal. Amos passed the full bucket to Nat Poindexter, his work buddy, and the Negro pitched the water out into the gob beyond the coal car tracks. Amos and Nat had laid those tracks themselves so that the coal cars, hauled in and out by the mules, could reach their room. It was what the miners called "dead work" as they weren't paid for it.

Amos and Nat had been working together since the summer. After the cave-in, Amos' former buddy, Marlon Styles, was so shaken he had quit the mine.

"I ain't never goin' back down there, Amos," Styles had told him. "And when I die, they can cremate me. I already done my time underground." Styles and his family moved up to Pittsburgh where his brother was employed by U.S. Steel. Amos had not heard from him since.

Nat Poindexter was new to the mine, but Amos had taken him as a buddy without complaint. Nat was a hard worker, strong, and best of all for Amos, quiet. Styles was a talker and had often irritated Amos by going on and on about anything that popped into his head. Even though few words were ever spoken between them, Amos and Nat had become good friends over the past months and had even gone fishing together a few times. Nat was a savvy angler with an uncanny sense of where fish were to be found. Their trips on the river had always produced a full basket of catfish and smallmouth bass.

Nat and his family lived with the other Negro families in a segregated patch at the very top of the ridge. They were paid the same wages as the white miners and their children were permitted to attend the Stewart School, but they were the first of the miners to be laid off when the mine slowed production.

The tight workspace was pitch dark except for the beams from the miners' lamps mounted on their helmets. Coal dust danced through the thin shafts of light giving them definition, and the shiny black coal seam glittered like broken glass. The miners were used to breathing in the coal dust, and amazingly it became a welcome feeling, almost like an addiction. There was a low rumble above the men that sounded like thunder.

"Roof is getting heavy," Amos said. He picked up a brass tipped sounding stick and tapped on the roof to judge its thickness. If it sounded "drummie" Amos would know the strata above them was separating. After twenty years on the job he had learned to interpret every groan, rumble and reverberation of the earth.

Amos had been mining coal since he was sixteen years old. He had followed his father Billy O'Neill into the mines in Western Pennsylvania. Billy himself had started at the age of nine as a "breaker boy," sorting coal from slag for twelve hours a day. Boys between the ages of eight and twelve sat inside the dusty breaker house on hard benches as a conveyor belt brought coal and slag down the chutes and between their legs. Their job was to pick the slate and other impurities from the coal. The boys were forbidden to wear gloves so that they could better handle the slick coal. As a result, fingers were constantly cut and bruised and sometimes even severed. Billy lost his baby finger at the age of ten. Some boys lost hands or feet, arms or legs when they were caught in the conveyor belts. The powerful machinery could drag a boy under and crush him to death, but even when that happened production would not stop. The mangled body would only be recovered at the end of the day. Eventually a separating machine replaced the breaker boys. Amos wasn't sure whether it was outrage or invention that had initiated the child labor laws.

Billy worked part-time now at the A&P in Steubenville. He suffered from coal worker's pneumoconiosis or what the men called "miner's asthma." The way Billy put it, after forty-six years in the mines his wind was "plum shot." He was slowly suffocating.

The rumbling overhead continued.

"We okay?" Nat asked.

Amos nodded.

A heavy roof was dangerous, but the downward pressure on the seam made the coal easy to cut, a condition they called a soft face. Amos turned his head and pointed his lamp into the gob. A pair of rats scurried away. The rats were a nuisance but their presence was a sign the space was safe.

Nat was superstitious about numbers. When he found out he was going to work in mine number six, it chilled his bones. This shaft had had its share of calamities since its opening, one gas explosion and two cave-ins in three years. That added up to ten dead and the loss of an arm, two feet, two eyes, and uncounted fingers. But Nat felt blessed to have drawn Amos as a buddy. He trusted Amos' instincts in the mine and admired his work ethic and his dry sense of humor. Once when they were "robbing pillars," a dangerous process where the columns of coal that were left to support a room are taken out one by one, Nat had started to cut down a pillar.

"Not that one." Amos had said. "We end up in the backyard of the church."

More than anything, Nat appreciated Amos' fairness. "He's not like the other white miners," Nat had told his wife Rose. "He don't spell Negro with a i and two g's."

The men were only half-finished bailing when they heard a tinkling harness bell. Fuzzy Totaro was coming up the shaft with his mule Jingles. Fuzzy stopped the mule in the entryway where the half empty coal cars were parked. He looked into the flooded room.

"You could drown a duck in here," Fuzzy said.

Amos nodded.

"Whaddaya wanna do?"

Amos shook his head. "Leave 'em and come back if you can. We're gonna work through lunch."

"I'll put the empties down at the cross. But you'll haf-ta push 'em up here yerselves. I'll see what I can do ta catch a trip in between."

"Thanks, Fuzzy." Amos said.

Jingles hee-hawed and lifted his head up and down. He kicked at the coal car behind him with a loud thump. Fuzzy jerked the reins.

"Keep yer shirt on, Jingles."

The ornery mule kicked the empty car again.

"I swear this jack was raised on sour milk."

Jingles was one of a dozen mules that lived full time in the darkness of the underground stables. Amos had always felt sorry for the animals who were taken above only to be shod or if they went lame or became ill. They had to be taken up at night or blindfolded to allow their eyes to adjust slowly to the daylight.

"I'll see you boys later," Fuzzy said. He led Jingles back down to the cross and unhitched the empty cars from the singletree, then stopped for a spell to breathe the mule. Amos and Nat went back to work.

It was another hour before the room was finally bailed out and the men could begin loading the cars. Amos hated mining "low coal." It required the men to work on their knees and in some narrower seams, to lay on their sides to shovel coal from the face. In a gassy mine like this, the shovelheads had to be made of brass so that they wouldn't cause a spark. The men tossed heavy shovels full of the black rock in an arc, bouncing it off the low roof and into the coal car. It was grueling work, but the men hurried to fill their cars. Fuzzy would be back soon to haul the cars to the main entry where they would be lifted to the surface by a powerful steam engine. There the coal would be weighed, then washed and separated by size: slack, nut, egg, and lump. Each miner had a metal chit they hung on their car so that the weigh boss could identify them as the loader and tally their tonnage.

Amos stopped shoveling and held up his hand. Nat froze and both men listened carefully. There was a soft cracking sound inside the face. Suddenly a huge chunk of the face fell down and more water gushed into the room filling it back up and soaking the men. Nat's shoulders slumped and he shook his head.

Amos squinted one eye. "How rare."

Mary tilted a white pitcher in the air and warm water poured out over Maureen's head. She squealed as the water rinsed the soap from her auburn hair. Maureen sat, arms crossed, in the large tin washtub in the middle of the kitchen floor. Mary was on her knees next to the steamy tub. She scooped more water warm up in the pitcher.

"It's in my eyes!" Maureen moaned.

"Oh, hush." Mary said and continued her rinsing. "One a these days Maureen, you'll learn that baths aren't punishment. Then God help us."

Annie and Lydia stood at the sink washing the supper dishes. They shared a smile. Molly and Isabelle were nestled in Mary's rocker next to the stove already bathed and dressed in their pajamas.

"Okay. Out," Mary said.

Maureen stood up shivering and Lydia brought over a warm towel and wrapped her sister in it. Maureen climbed out of the tub and quickly moved across the newspapers in front of the warm stove.

Mary sat back on her haunches next to the tub, and wiped her brow with her forearm. She sighed, and looked over at Annie.

"Let's go."

Annie nodded and began undressing. Lydia brought the copper boiler from the stove and poured more hot water into the tin tub to warm it up. When Annie finished, it would be Lydia's turn. Then they all would go upstairs while Loy had his bath in private. The tub would be cleaned and emptied and more water would be heated in the boiler for Amos' bath when he came home from work.

Mary had promised that after their baths the children would be allowed to listen to the radio for another hour before bed. Each of them had their favorite program. Loy's was *The Lone Ranger*, which came on at 4:30 in the afternoon. The kids always listened to it after school. Annie loved it too, but her favorite show was *One Man's Family* on Sunday evening. Tonight there would be Christmas music, and as Annie sat in the tin tub bathing herself, she felt her anxiousness growing. Would she get to meet Santa tonight or would her hopes be dashed at the last minute by being sent to bed with the other children?

After Loy's bath he joined his mother and sisters in the living room.

Mary had turned on the radio and *Silent Night* was playing softly. Isabelle and Molly were on each side of Mary snuggled in tight, and Lydia was sitting cross-legged on the rug knitting. Baby Faith was already asleep in the little cradle by the Franklin stove. Loy moved over next to Annie on the old couch and Pepper curled up at his feet. Annie took Loy's hand and squeezed it. He smiled at her and squeezed back. Loy knew he wasn't supposed to have a favorite sister, but he did. When he looked over at Maureen, she made a face at him. And there was no doubt in his mind who should get the boobie prize.

The Announcer came on the Radio. "You're listening to songs for the Christmas Season on station KDKA, broadcasting from Pittsburgh, Pennsylvania. We're going to join President Roosevelt now, live on the CBS network, from the Capitol in Washington, D.C., for his Christmas address to the nation."

As Annie stared at the glowing dial of the radio, the President's voice came on. That deep, comforting voice they had all learned to trust. Amos had told his children in no uncertain terms, President Roosevelt had saved the country.

"Once more the most joyous of all days draws near," Roosevelt began, *"and again it is my great privilege on this blessed Eve of the Nativity to wish the American people everywhere a Merry Christmas."*

"Is that Santa Claus, Mommy?" Isabelle asked.

"No, honey. It's the President."

"This is the third time that I have joined in these Christmas Eve festivities," Roosevelt continued. *"We are gathered together in a typical American setting in the park here in front of the White House. Before me and around me is an American assemblage... men and women of all ages, youths and maidens, young children who know nothing about the cares of life... all jubilant with joyous expectation.*

"The night has fallen and the spirit of other days, too, broods over the scene. Andrew Jackson looks down upon us from his prancing steed; and the four corners of the square in which we are gathered around a gaily lit Christmas tree are guarded by the figures of intrepid leaders in the Revolutionary War... Von Steuben, the German; Kosciusko, the Pole; and Lafayette and Rochambeau from the shores of France.

"This is in keeping with the universal spirit of the festival we are celebrating; for we who stand here among our guardians out of the past and from far shores are, I suppose, as diverse in blood and origin as are the uncounted millions throughout the land to whom these words go out tonight. But around the Manger of the Babe of Bethlehem all Nations and kindreds and tongues find unity. For the spirit of Christmas knows no race, no creed, no clime, no limitation of time or space.

"The spirit of Christmas breathes an eternal message of peace and good-will to all men. We pause therefore on this Holy Night and, laying down the burdens and the cares of life and casting aside the anxieties of the common day, rejoice that nineteen hundred years ago, heralded by angels, there came into the world One whose message was of peace, who gave to all mankind a new commandment of love."

There was a loud knock on the front door. Pepper hopped to his feet and barked. Mary looked puzzled and Loy got up and ran over to the door.

The President concluded, *"And so I greet you with the greeting of the Angels on that first Christmas at Bethlehem which, resounding through centuries, still rings out with its eternal message: Glory to God in the highest, and on earth peace and good will to men."*

When Loy opened the door, Pepper dashed out. Loy turned back, and a big smile came to his face.

"Ma. Come look."

Out on the porch, a group of miners, their wives and children began singing. *"We Three Kings of Orient are, Bearing gifts we travel afar. Field and fountain moor and mountain following yonder star."*

Mary and the children crowded around the door. When Lydia peeked out she almost gasped. John Travis, a good looking sandy haired boy of fifteen was part of the gaily dressed chorus. He smiled broadly at Lydia as he sang and she ducked quickly behind her mother, mortified.

The O'Neills' neighbors in the duplex, the Tulacs, were at their door, and Mrs. Tulac smiled and waved to Mary. Mr. Tulac came out on the porch grinning ear to ear.

Annie smiled as John Travis leaned to the side to try and see Lydia. Annie elbowed her sister and Lydia fluffed her hair back with her hands and peeked out from behind her mother. She waved shyly to the boy and John Travis beamed. When the carol ended, everyone applauded. Mr. Tulac clapped loudest and spoke in his thick Hungarian accent, "Sank you so much. Dis is beautiful."

"Merry Christmas," Mary added.

Merry Christmases echoed around the porch.

John Travis stepped forward as the group moved on. "Merry Christmas, Lydia."

"Merry Christmas, John."

All the kids were staring at John. "I didn't know ya had such a big family."

"There's seven of us," Annie offered. "All boys, except for six."

Mary's eyes went wide. "Annie!"

"That's what Daddy said."

"Is he the boy yer sweet on?" Isabelle asked tugging at Lydia's robe.

Lydia's face flushed. Mary was biting her lip to hold back her smile. Even John Travis was blushing.

"Well, I guess I'll see ya at school," he said.

Lydia nodded.

"Good night… and Merry Christmas."

"Merry Christmas," they all said.

John hurried off the porch to catch up with his group. They were already knocking on the Patterson's door. Mr. Tulac held up a finger to Mary.

"Don't go. I come back."

Mr. Tulac disappeared into his house for a moment and came back out with a bottle of his homemade elderberry wine. He handed it to Mary.

"For you and Amos. Merry Christmas."

"Ya didn't have to do that, Stefan," Mary said.

"Is my pleasure."

Mary held up the bottle. "I know Amos will enjoy this."

The moon came out of the clouds and lit up the snow covered landscape in soft blue light. It was almost as bright as day. Annie stepped out on the porch as Mrs. Tulac and Mary exchanged a hug. Annie stared off at the northern horizon. He's coming, she thought. Annie could hardly stand still.

All the children watched as their mother came up from the kitchen with a plate of cookies and a glass of milk for Santa. She set them on the side table.

"He'll see it, won't he, Mama?" Molly asked.

"He always does." Mary shared a look with Annie and they both smiled.

"Is Uncle Butch comin' tomorra?" Loy asked.

"Yes… And I don't want you expectin' presents as soon as he steps in the door. It's been a hard year for 'em."

Maureen crossed her arms over her chest. "How comes Daddy has to work on Christmas?"

"To make things better for us," Mary said. "To be honest, he doesn't have a choice."

"He sounded real mad," Maureen said.

Mary gathered the children around the Franklin stove.

"Yes, he was angry. But he had every right to be. Annie asked me today if Daddy was mad at us. He's not. He loves all-a-ya."

The children listened intently to their mother.

"Yer father is a quiet man. But just because a person is quiet, doesn't mean they don't have deep feelins. Do you understand?"

Annie sat on the couch and nodded her head slowly. The music on the radio ended and the announcer came back on.

"I hope you're enjoying our songs for the Christmas season. We'll be getting back to them shortly, but as I promised, we're going to see if we can reach the North Pole. Let's see now... We'll turn on this old short wave."

There was the sound of static and then a high-pitched whistle.

"Santa? Can you hear us? Come in Santa..."

There was more static and the sound of wind.

"Santa... are you there?"

The children were transfixed. Annie walked closer to the radio. The static disappeared and the radio went silent. Then suddenly a basso profundo voice burst from the tiny speaker.

"HO, HO, HO!"

"That's him!" Maureen said.

"Merr-rry Christmas! HO, HO, HO!"

"Merry Christmas to you, Santa," the announcer said. "How are things at the North Pole?"

"Oh Splendid, Tim. We're all ready to go. The elves have packed up the sleigh and the reindeer are all hitched up. I don't believe I've ever seen them so excited!"

Isabelle squealed and almost fell off her chair. Molly clapped her hands. Annie shushed them.

"Well, it sounds as if everything is on schedule."

Santa chuckled. "Yes indeed. Mrs. Claus has made sure of that."

Mary's eyes were closed but a smile came to her lips.

"Santa, do you have a message for all the boys and girls listening tonight?"

"Yes I do, Tim... Children, always listen to what your Mother and Father tell you. When you're good boys and girls, you make Santa very happy. HO, HO, HO!"

"Well, we don't want to take up anymore of your time, Santa. We know how busy you're going to be tonight."

"Yes, I must be going. But before I do, I want to wish everyone a very Merry Christmas! HO, HO, HO!... HO, HO, HO!"

There was a crackle and static and the sound of wind as Santa's voice faded out. Mary smiled and switched off the radio.

"All right," she said. "It's time for bed."

Maureen looked up at her Mother, distressed. "Ohhh... Not yet, Mama."

"Let's go. Upstairs."

Annie sat rigid on the couch. She knew this was the moment of truth. Maureen looked at Annie then back at her mother.

"It's too early for bed."

"Didn't you hear what Santa said? Move it, Missy."

The other girls started toward the steps. Mary herded Maureen in that direction. Annie looked over at Lydia who had taken up her knitting again. Loy was petting Pepper. Neither one of them was moving. Annie held her breath. When her mother reached the steps she turned back.

"Annie, you get the baby."

Annie went rigid. Was she being sent to bed?

Her mother started up the stairs and it was all Annie could do to stand. Neither Lydia nor Loy was paying any attention to her. Annie was in a panic. She picked the sleeping baby up from the cradle and carried her upstairs.

Annie went into her parents' room and laid Faith in her crib at the foot of Mama's bed. She covered her baby sister with a blanket and a knitted afghan, tucking them up close to the sleeping child's chin. She leaned down and kissed the baby's cheek. When she came out of the bedroom Annie stood near the top of the stairs. I should go back downstairs, she thought. I did what Mama asked me to. But she couldn't get her feet to move. She was frozen in the spot.

Annie looked into her bedroom and saw Isabelle and Molly pile into the little bed. Mary pulled the covers up around them and kissed each one. Maureen stood by the side of the big bed.

"Let's go, Missy. Hop in," Mary said.

Maureen looked out the door and saw Annie in the hall. "What about her?"

As her mother turned to look out at her, Annie's heart sank.

"Annie is gonna stay up and help me tonight," Mary said. A thrill went through Annie like she never felt before. She'd made it!

"Can't I stay up, too? I'm almost ten."

"Climb in."

"I wanna meet Santa Claus."

Mary pulled the covers down and guided the protesting child into the big bed.

"This ain't fair."

"Hush now."

Mary pulled the covers back up and gave Maureen a kiss.

"Can I stay up next year, Mama?"

"Maybe. We'll see."

Maureen's eyes lit up and a big smile broke across her face. She threw her arms around her mother and hugged her hard.

"Now you go right to sleep if you want Santa to come."

"Yes, Mama," the children answered.

Maureen looked out the door and smiled at Annie. Mary went out of the room and closed the door. Maureen lay back in the big bed glowing.

"I'm gonna stay up next year." Maureen announced.

"Mama said maybe."

Maureen just smiled.

Mary came down into the kitchen followed by Lydia, Loy, and Annie. The newspapers that were on the floor had been picked up and replaced by scatter rugs. Mary walked to her rocking chair and sat down heavily. She'd been up and working since 5:00 a.m. Loy stood by the pine table. He was raring to go.

"Should we get started now?" he asked.

Mary shook her head. "No. I'm gonna rest my eyes for an hour." She leaned back in the chair and her eyes closed. Lydia held a finger to her lips, and Annie nodded. Loy looked disappointed.

"Why don't you play Chinese checkers for a while?" Lydia whispered.

Annie nodded and Loy went to fetch the game. He walked quietly to the cupboard.

"Mama."

Mary's eyes popped open and the children turned toward the steps. Molly stood at the bottom of the stairs, one hand between her legs.

"I haf-ta go."

Mary sighed heavily and started to get up.

"I'll take her, Mama." Lydia said.

Lydia took Molly's hand and led her to the coat rack, where they both bundled up. Lydia stepped into her boots, picked Molly up and opened the back door.

Pepper raced in and shook himself and went over to sit near the stove. Annie watched through the window as Lydia carried their little sister down the path to the outhouse. The moon was higher now, a big bright gibbous moon, perfect for navigating the river valley. A shiver ran down Annie's back. She was going to see reindeer fly!

Amos and Nat pushed the empty cars up from the track crossing and Amos jammed sprags, pieces of wood about eighteen inches long and two inches thick, in through the spokes of the wheels to keep the cars from rolling back. Amos leaned back against the car to catch his breath. They had been working nonstop for eight hours. The bandage on Amos' finger had gotten soaked and fallen off. His hand ached and his bad shoulder was sore from all the bailing.

"Les eat, huh," Nat said.

Amos nodded.

Nat got their buckets and the men wolfed down their food. Nat had his usual, beans and cornbread. He leaned back against the coal car as he ate, his eyes closed.

"I'm bushed," Nat said. "I ain't gettin' no sleep. One of them babies wakes up the other one."

Amos knew that Nat's neighbor, Oscar Bennett, had been fired by the company. "O" had gone on a bender and then disappeared three weeks ago, leaving his wife Lenore and their newborn baby on their own. The company officially fired "O" on Monday. On Tuesday an Iron and Coal policeman came to evict Lenore from the patch.

Lenore and her baby had nowhere to go. Rose tearfully pleaded with Nat to take them in. He had agreed even though he knew he could not afford to feed them.

"And that ain't the worst of it," Nat said. "Lenore's milk has dried up from the worry. Rose is nursing her baby and Nat junior."

Amos could only shake his head.

"I don't know what to do," Nat said.

"You're doin' it."

When Amos found the oatmeal cookies at the bottom of his growler both men smiled. Nat loved Mary's cookies, pies, and cakes. The cookies quickly disappeared.

"Mmmmm. She's quite the baker," Nat said.

Amos nodded and smiled. He moved around to try and get comfortable.

"Howd-ja meet her?"

"Armistice Day dance at the American Legion."

"She from Steubenville?"

Amos nodded. "Her brother Ray was a good friend a mine. I guess she took pity on me."

"She knew."

Amos shrugged. "I was dull as dishwater."

Amos had come home from the Great War in 1919, rail-thin and lucky to be alive. Amos fought in the bloody battle of the Belleau Wood. Upon arrival at the front, Amos' captain, Lloyd Williams, was informed of the danger of the situation and ordered by the French commander to retreat. Williams' reply would make him famous, '*Retreat hell, we just got here,*' he said. The battle lasted for three weeks and the fighting was so fierce the Germans named the U.S. Marines "Devil Dogs." By the time the battle ended nearly ten thousand Marines were dead. Captain Williams was killed, but Amos survived, only to be stricken with influenza. Shell shocked and near death, he lay in a French hospital for two months before he was strong enough to ship home. The flu pandemic was the worst in history infecting forty million people, and three times the number that fell in the Great War.

Mary saw Amos for the first time when her brother Ray pointed him out, standing alone in a corner of the Legion Hall gymnasium. Amos was wearing his father's suit and it hung loosely on him. Mary came over and introduced herself. Amos was polite but distant. Mary looked lovely that night. She was wearing her best dress and had just had a hair bob by her friend Arlene who was going to beautician school in Wheeling. When Mary realized their conversation wasn't going anywhere, she took the bold move of asking Amos to dance. He shook his head, "No, thank you."

Mary stared at him for a moment. "You don't know how, do you?"

"No, Ma'am, I don't."

"I can teach ya."

Mary reached out and took his hand. Her smile was warm and her blue eyes were shining. Amos thought Mary was pretty, and those blue eyes didn't miss much. They were intelligent, and kind. And her temperament was as mild as milk.

"It's easy. You'll see," she said. Mary gently drew him out on the dance floor, and over the next months gently drew him back into the world.

There was a distant look in Amos' eye as Nat watched him eat the last cookie.

"You never talk about the war," Nat said.

Amos just shook his head.

Loy stared down at the homemade Chinese checkerboard, his lips pursed and his eyes narrow. The board was a square piece of wood with holes drilled in it. Beans served as the playing pieces, white and black. Annie and Loy were in the middle of their game and Loy was studying the board intently. He only had four beans left. His sister had ten. Annie looked around the kitchen. Mama was asleep in her rocking chair. Pepper was curled up on the rug by the stove. She looked up at the electric clock. It was 11:30.

Loy seemed to have a revelation and finally made his move. He looked up at Annie and raised his eyebrows. She was not really interested in the game. There were too many other things on her mind. She glanced down at the board for a moment and then moved a bean. She yawned, then looked to see that no one caught it. Lydia was at the other end of the table reading her library book, *A Tale of Two Cities*.

Loy made his next move quickly. Annie looked down, then multiple jumped Loy's last men. He was stunned.

"I can't believe it. Who taught ya to play so good!?"

Mary opened her eyes and looked at the children. "If ya wanna shout, Loyal, go outside and do it. There's children sleeping."

Mary slowly got out of her chair and went to the china closet. She opened a drawer. "Clean that up now."

Loy was still shaking his head. He picked up the game and put it away. Mary brought a shiny red oilcloth and spread it over the pine table. It was the only bright color in the whole kitchen and it gave a festive tone to an otherwise dreary room.

Mary and Lydia exchanged smiles.

"Loy, get the things from the cellar."

Annie watched, unsure of what was going to happen next, for she was very excited. Her mother got the good dishes out and stacked them on the red oilcloth. Lydia was looking for something in the high cabinet.

Loy came back through the curtain from the cellar carrying a large bag. He brought it to the table and began to unpack it. There were big red, delicious apples, thick-skinned oranges, and a huge bunch of bananas! Annie couldn't believe it.

Lydia came down from the high cabinet with a smaller bag and emptied cream candy, hard tack, and a box of chocolates onto the table. Lydia smiled and Annie could hardly hide her surprise. Mary refilled the copper boiler at the sink and then put it on the stove. She bent to shovel more coal into the firebox from the kitchen coal bin.

Lydia took one of dishes from the stack and began filling it with a piece of each kind of fruit, and a selection of candy.

"The oranges are so big this year," she said.

Loy took a plate and began to fill it as Lydia started another.

He held up an orange. "Look at this one."

Annie was wide-eyed. "Where'd they come from?"

"The store," Loy said. "Come on. You can make one."

Annie moved in closer and took a plate. She copied what her brother and sister were doing. Soon all seven plates were loaded with Christmas goodies.

Mary nodded her approval. "Ya can each have one piece a candy."

The children selected one chocolate a piece from the box. Annie was confused, but delighted. Pepper sat up suddenly and barked.

Mary scolded the dog. "SHHHHHH."

They heard footsteps on the back porch and then Amos came into the kitchen and quickly shut the door. His face was so black that even his mustache was invisible. He was covered with coal dust from head to toe.

"Hey, Pop!" Loy said.

When Amos smiled, the contrast between his white teeth and his black face made everyone laugh. He kept his voice low, but his excitement was clear.

"Hello, kids. Merry Christmas!"

"Merry Christmas, Daddy," Lidia said.

The children rushed to assist him in removing his sooty clothes. Amos undid his tool belt and hung it on the hook. Lydia took his heavy coat and Loy began working on his boots. Amos' wet overalls were frozen stiff from the walk up the hill from the mine. Annie stepped up shyly and took his pit helmet and her Daddy smiled at her.

Amos looked over at the red tablecloth and the fruit plates. "It looks like Santa's already been here."

Annie tried to smile. She was so nervous she thought she would bust. Pepper ran over and jumped up on Amos.

"Down, boy. I'm filthy," he said. But Amos petted the dog anyway.

He walked to the sink and turned on the cold water, washed his hands and then bristled as the icy water hit his face. He had to scrub hard to get the coal dust out of his skin.

Mary pulled the tin tub back into the middle of the kitchen floor. "Go upstairs now while your father gets his bath," she said. "Take a plate with ya."

They each picked up a plate from the table and Loy led the way up the stairs.

Amos sat in the little tub with his knees tight to his chest as Mary bathed him tenderly. Her fingers slid over the jagged scar on his left shoulder which had been broken during the cave in. The muscles were tight here and Amos sighed as she massaged him.

"I need you to talk to Loyal. He went off sled riding with Alden Reese and didn't come home until nearly five o'clock. He was meant to be home at eleven. I know it's Christmas but I won't be disobeyed like that."

Amos nodded his head. "I'll talk to him." He let his chin drop to his chest and he closed his eyes.

"Tired?" she asked.

"Some."

"There's lots a work to be done."

"It's not work."

Mary put her arms around him and hugged him. "I love you, Amos."

Annie stood at the front door as Loy dragged the blue spruce tree in from the porch. She quickly closed the door then joined Lydia, helping their brother place the stump into the Christmas tree stand in the corner of the living room. Loy turned the tree until the fullest side was showing.

"Whaddaya think?" he asked.

"Perfect," Lydia answered.

Annie had a growing feeling of unease. "When do ya think he's gonna get here?"

"Huh?" Loy looked over at his sister. "Oh, he won't be long. Mama will make sure a that. Then the real fun's gonna start."

Annie shivered with excitement. Lydia put her arm around Annie. "Isn't it a pretty tree?"

"It sure is." Annie hugged her big sister. "This is gonna be the best Christmas ever."

Mary came up the stairs with a pitcher of water. Her look was stern. "Loyal, yer father wants to see ya downstairs."

Loy hung his head. "Yes, ma'am." He shared a worried look with Annie and walked slowly to the stairs and went down.

Mary knelt by the tree and poured the pitcher of water into the little reservoir of the Christmas tree stand.

"Mama?" Annie asked. "Is Loy gonna get a whippin'?"

Mary sighed and looked up at her. "I 'spect he is." Mary didn't look happy about it.

Annie sat down on the couch. She was sleepy and her stomach felt upset. It had been such a long day already and the biggest part was still to come. Her eyes were getting heavy, but she didn't dare close them for fear she would fall asleep. She felt terrible for Loy. Getting a whippin' when Santa was coming. How much longer would they have to wait? What if Santa didn't come to their house until the wee hours. Would she be able to stay awake? She would never forgive herself if she fell asleep and missed him. The young girl leaned back on the couch and rubbed her eyes.

The sound of sleigh bells made Annie's eyes pop open. She looked toward the stairs, and her smile turned to a look of amazement.

"Ho, Ho, Ho…"

A big stack of boxes appeared, dancing up the stairs toward the living room.

"Ho, Ho, Ho!"

Annie rose slowly from the couch. Her feet shuffled and she didn't know what to do with her hands. Oh my, she thought. It's him! It's Santa!

The boxes entered the living room and a face peeked out from behind them. Amos smiled out at Annie and raised his bushy eyebrows. Annie felt her shoulders slump. Loy came up the stairs behind his father carrying two shopping bags. Lydia ran over to help them. She took a stack of boxes from her father and piled them near the tree. Mary took the shopping bags from Loy but he didn't look her in the eye.

Annie put her hand to her heart. She was just a little annoyed that she had been fooled. Loy opened a box that contained the Christmas decorations.

"Careful now. Those bulbs are fragile," Amos said.

Annie walked over slowly and looked down into the box. Loy pulled out a string of colored electric lights and started to unwind the coil.

"We start with these. We haf-ta space 'em out just right," Loy said.

Annie nodded. All this time she had thought that Santa decorated their tree. But of course, with all the work he had to do that night, didn't it made sense for the family to help him?

Lydia opened another box that contained colored glass balls and a homemade chain of popcorn. Annie knelt down with Loy and helped him stretch out the string of lights.

Amos spread a white sheet under the tree and carefully placed small boxes and pieces of curved wood under it to create a mountain and a plain. He started laying the tracks of the electric train that would circle the tree.

Annie helped her brother string the electric Christmas lights around the tree, fastening each of them to the thin branches. Lydia hung the colored glass balls and then added the popcorn chain. Soon the tree was sparkling with decorations. Lydia got a chair from the dining room and put the Angel on the treetop.

Amos seemed to be enjoying himself immensely. He whistled softly as he unpacked the creche. He placed the little wooden stable under the tree and put some straw inside it. The figures of Mary and Joseph were set on each side of a small cradle where a baby Jesus lay. Inside and around the stable he placed the farm animals, and finally, the Three Wise Men.

"Loy, get me some ashes from the bucket."

Loy ran to the Franklin stove and collected some ashes in the top of a shoebox and carried them back to his father.

Using a teaspoon and his finger, Amos painstakingly began sprinkling the ashes to give contour to the mountain and plain and make paths to and from the stable. It was like he was making a painting.

It looked beautiful to Annie, but she had a growing feeling of unease. She looked over at her mother. Mary reached into a shopping bag and took out three small, homemade Raggedy Ann dolls. They had striped stockings and red yarn for hair. Mary had sat up nights making them from scraps of cloth and buttons.

"I'll help ya wrap." Lydia said.

Annie watched as Lydia pulled a white dress out of the other shopping bag. "I remember this. Who's it for now?

"Molly."

As Lydia began to wrap the dress in green tissue paper, Annie felt like she was sinking. It was slowly dawning on her what was happening. She walked to the window and stared out. The wind was howling through the hollow. The snow had turned to sleet and the moon was obscured by dark black clouds. Tears formed in Annie's eyes.

Amos sat back and surveyed his work. He smiled contentedly.

"Plug her in, son."

Loy plugged the string of lights in and the Christmas tree bloomed in color. Amos placed a silver foil star on one of the electric lights that hung over the creche.

Amos looked up at Mary. "Waddaya think?"

Mary smiled. "It's beautiful."

Annie turned from the window as her father got up and walked to the side table where the milk and cookies had been left for Santa. He looked so happy. Amos took one of the cookies and popped it into his mouth. When he chugged down the milk, Annie turned back to the window. She was sobbing heavily now.

Amos had almost drained the milk when he saw that Annie was crying. He turned to his wife.

"Mary…"

Mary and Lydia looked up from their wrapping and saw Annie crying.

"What's wrong, child?" Mary asked.

"You tricked me! You all tricked me! Santa Claus isn't coming! You've done everything he was s'posed ta do! The tree, the fruit plates, the gifts… He's never coming!" Tears streamed down the young girl's cheeks. "There is no Santa Claus, is there?"

Amos turned to Mary. "Didn't ya tell her?"

"I thought she knew."

"You lied to me. Everyone lied. Even the radio!"

Lydia hurried to Annie's side. "Annie… Daddy is Santa Claus."

Annie was crying hard now. She looked at her father in disbelief. "You're not Santa Claus. You're nothing like him!"

Amos was chilled to the bone.

"Annie!" Mary started toward her daughter, but Annie ran past her, past her father and up the stairs. Amos looked up the stairs after her, and then hung his head.

Annie pulled the covers back on the big bed and slid in next to the window. She was still crying. Maureen was sleeping peacefully on the other side of the bed. Annie looked over at her little sisters snuggled under the thick blanket in the little bed. The poor things, Annie thought. Wait 'til they find out. It'll kill 'em. She wiped away the tears and shook her head. It was all clear as a bell now. How could she have been so stupid? She had ignored "Rotten Alan" Tuttle when he bragged in the schoolyard that there was no Santa Claus. She had ignored the question in her own mind of how one sleigh could hold enough toys for all the boys and girls in the world, not to mention the impossible task of delivering them all in one night. And she had even ignored the fact that the foreman's children always got better presents from Santa than the poorer kids. Did Santa like rich children better? No! There was no Santa Claus. And the world was a darker place now. Annie bit down on her lip to keep from sobbing out loud. This was the worst Christmas of her life. And Christmas would never be the same again.

Loy stood up and yawned. "I'm goin' ta bed. Come on, Pepper." Loy walked to the dining room door. "I'll see yins in the mornin'. Merry Christmas."

They wished him a Merry Christmas and he closed the door.

"Good night, Mama. Don't worry. I'll talk to her." Lydia kissed her mother and Mary nodded.

Lydia kissed her father. "Good night, Daddy. I love you."

Lydia climbed the stairs leaving her mother and father alone. Amos sighed and sat down heavily in his chair. Mary came over and sat on the arm. She ran her fingers slowly through his thick black hair.

"She didn't mean it, honey. She was upset."

Amos just nodded.

"I'm sorry I told you about Loy. You didn't whip him did ya?"

"No." Amos looked up at his wife. "He wasn't sled ridin'. He was pickin' coal from the clume."

"What?"

"He wanted to make some money so he could buy ya a present."

"Me?"

Amos nodded. Tears formed in Mary's eyes. "Oh Lord. That boy."

Amos pulled Mary down into his lap.

"I'm too heavy," she protested.

"Not for me you ain't." Amos pulled her tight.

He looked over at the wrapped presents under the tree.

"It ain't much."

"More than a lot of folks."

She touched his cheek and his rough hand covered hers.

"It's coming on a new year. Maybe it'll be a better one," he said.

"We'll pray it is."

Mary climbed off his lap and helped pull her weary husband to his feet. "Why don't-cha go to bed. I got a few more things to put out for the older ones. Before ya know it those kids are gonna be screamin'.

Annie lay in bed facing the window, her back to the room. She closed her eyes when she heard Lydia come in and pretended to be sleeping. Lydia climbed into the big bed next to her.

"Annie... Annie..."

Annie opened her eyes, but she didn't answer.

"Are you awake?" There was no response, but Lydia continued. "I'm sorry, Annie. I thought-cha knew. It's okay. Christmas is still Christmas."

Annie just stared at the window, blinking back tears. Outside a vicious wind was battering sleet against the pane. Lydia sighed softly. She leaned in and kissed Annie's shoulder, then rolled over and closed her eyes.

The weight of the day had taken its toll on Annie. She didn't want to go to sleep, but she couldn't hold her eyes open another minute. A moment after they closed she drifted into a deep slumber.

When Annie awoke, the room was still dark. She sat up in bed and listened. The house was quiet and the wind had stopped howling. The moon was still up and it made just enough cold light for her to see that all her sisters were still fast asleep. Annie felt horrible. She got out from underneath the covers carefully and slipped out of bed.

Annie tiptoed down the hall past her parents' room. She could hear her father snoring softly. She went down the stairs quietly and into the living room. The moonlight was brighter here and Annie walked to the tree and found the plug for the Christmas lights. When she plugged them in the tree came alight in a burst of color.

There were presents under the tree. The fruit plates, homemade dolls and hand-me-down dresses she had seen her mother wrapping. There was also a brand new Monopoly game. She knew Loy would be delighted.

Annie knelt down by the glowing tree and surveyed her father's work. The ash-colored mountain and the plain, the stable with the wise men. Mary and Joseph and baby Jesus bedding down with the cows and the sheep, with the shining star of Bethlehem over them. All the things she had thought Santa would do had been done by her father, a quiet man who was as far from a jolly Saint Nick as she could imagine. But as she stared at the tiny village he had created the realization of her harsh words to him made tears come to her eyes. She had questioned in her mind if her father was angry with his children or if they were a burden to him. But tonight she understood more about him than she ever did before, and she loved him with all her heart. How awful she had been to him tonight. Tears rolled down the young girl's cheeks, but slowly she crossed the threshold from pain to a quiet joy.

As Annie stood there by the lighted tree she understood for the first time the true meaning of Christmas. It isn't what's inside those packages, she thought; Christmas is in your heart.

And what about Santa Claus? Was he just a made up character? No… She had heard about St. Nicolas in her Sunday school class. He was a rich man and he had given away everything he had to the poor. Mrs. Meyers told the class the story of St. Nicolas tossing a bag of gold through the window of a poor and needy family. The gold landed in the children's shoes and stockings. And that's why we hang stockings up at Christmas today. St. Nicolas was the patron saint of children, a real person, like Jesus. Children all over the world believed in him. Didn't their belief bring with it boundless joy? Annie had felt that joy. It was real. And all the parents who stay up late to wrap the presents for their children, they felt that joy too. Annie had seen it in her father's and mother's eyes—the joy of giving. A joy that takes on even more grace because the giving is done without claiming credit for it. Santa Claus exists, all right, Annie thought. And she knew just where to find him.

Annie went back up the stairs quietly and walked to her parents' room. She listened for a moment, then slowly opened the door. Her bare feet crossed the wooden floor to the bed where her father and mother were sleeping peacefully. Annie checked on Faith, making sure the baby's covers were snug. Then she stood there for a long moment at the bottom of the bed watching her Father sleep.

Annie stepped closer, her mind rolling over what she had been practicing for weeks. When she was ready, she reached over and shook her father's arm gently.

"Daddy."

Amos woke up suddenly, startled out of his sleep. He looked surprised and confused. "What's a matter? Is everything all right?"

Annie nodded. "I wanted ta tell ya somethin'."

Amos stared at her as Annie stood up as straight and tall as she could.

"Thank you for all the wonderful presents you bring us every year."

Amos looked confused. There were tears in Annie's eyes now.

"Daddy, I'm glad you're Santa Claus."

Annie threw her arms around her father and kissed his cheek. She turned then and ran out of the room.

Amos shook his head in wonder. A wide smile came to his face as he lay back on his pillow. He closed his eyes again, but the smile remained.

CHRISTMAS DAY

Maureen jumped on Annie's side of the bed and shook her hard. "It's Christmas! Wake up! It's Christmas!"

Lydia whacked Maureen with a pillow but it didn't have the least bit of an effect on the excited child. Maureen hopped over to the little bed and woke up Isabelle and Molly.

Annie opened her eyes just in time to see her sister roar out the door.

"Mama, Daddy! Wake up! It's Christmas!"

The day had dawned cloudless and cold and the sky turned cobalt blue. The sleet had left an ice sheen on the entire landscape. The bare trees looked like they were sculpted of glass.

The O'Neills were gathered around the lighted Christmas tree; the kids were on the floor opening presents, wrapping paper flying. Mary and Amos sat in their chairs, smiling. Loy had the top off the Monopoly game. He was grinning like the Cheshire cat.

Isabelle was already eating candy from her fruit plate. Maureen unwrapped her Raggedy Ann doll and squealed with delight. "Oh, she's beautiful!" Maureen hugged the doll to her chest. But when her happy little sisters unwrapped their dolls, Maureen looked a bit annoyed and immediately began comparing whose doll was bigger.

Annie unwrapped her gift. It was a small basket with a lid that fastened with a clasp. Inside it were spools of thread, needles, a thimble, scissors and a pattern for a new dress. Annie was delighted!

Loy reached under the tree and brought his mother's present out. He shyly handed the little red bag over to her. Amos was smiling broadly. Mary opened the bag and pulled out the gold jar of cold cream. Tears filled Mary's eyes. She unscrewed the lid and took in the aroma. "Lavender," she said. "It's my favorite."

Loy was glowing now. Mary bent down and kissed him and he hugged her hard.

"Better look in your stocking, Buster," she said.

Loy eyes lit up and he ran to where the stockings were hanging by the Franklin stove. He took his stocking down and saw it was filled with coal. Loy shook his head.

"Very funny."

Loy dumped the stocking full of coal out into the bin by the stove and a brand new silver dollar landed on the top of the pile. Loy was stunned. He looked over at his mother and she just nodded.

"I imagine you'd like to see a movie, the way you go on about it all the time," Mary said.

Loy ran back to his mother and gave her a hug and kiss.

"I love you mum." There were tears in the boy's eyes.

"I love you too."

Molly squealed as she opened the package that contained her "new" white dress. She held it up smiling, still clutching her doll. "Look, Annie! Look what Santa brought for me!"

"It's beautiful!" Annie said. The dress had been Annie's when she was Molly's age.

The mention of Santa Claus made Maureen turn. Her eyes went wide and she swooped in on Annie.

"Did ya meet Santa last night?" Maureen asked.

Mary and Amos overheard Maureen's question. They both looked at Annie. All the children turned to Annie expectantly.

"I saw him alright," Annie said

Maureen could hardly sit still. "What did ya say?"

A smile came to Annie's face. "I thanked him for all of us," she said.

Annie turned to her father. He was smiling too. He couldn't have been more proud of her. Amos winked at Annie… and Annie winked back. Mary put her arm around her husband and he turned to her and they kissed.

The front door opened and Billy O'Neill stepped in. "Merry Christmas!" The old man was out of breath from the long walk up the hill but his voice was full of joy. And he was carrying a Christmas ham the size of a football!

"Grandpa!" the children exclaimed. "Merry Christmas."

Billy passed the ham off to Mary and she hugged and kissed him.

Loy held up his present. "I got a Monopoly game, Grandpa."

"Well, I see Santa was good to you kids," Billy said.

Annie smiled and nodded and sat back on her heels. She looked around at her happy family. Some of the magic of youth had been surrendered by her passage through this season, but it was replaced by a deeper understanding that glowed in her heart. The spirit of Christmas is love, Annie thought. Love, and family and the joy of giving.

Molly crawled into Annie's lap. "Whadd-ja git, Annie?"

Annie smiled. "It's a new sewing basket. Now I can make my own dress."

"Oooo, you lucky dog."

Annie hugged her little sister hard. "Amen," she said.

ACKNOWLEDGEMENTS

I have a boatload of people to thank, more numerous than can be mentioned here, I'm afraid. I could start with my fourth-grade teacher, Miss Elliot. But then this would run on to more pages than the story in this book. Suffice it to say that I have received encouragement in my lifetime from family and friends, mentors and critics… Encouragement is a powerful thing. It is literally the light at the end of the tunnel.

I want to thank Kim Dawson and Tim Moore, compatriots in all my work, for their friendship, insight, and support; Greg Taylor, a great writer and a partner on other projects and my brother Rick, who always had and has my back.

I married Toni Semple thirty-five years ago. I cannot overstate the advantage it is to marry someone smarter than you. Her love and support is the foundation of my life. My stepson Noah Coleman has enriched our lives and I am grateful for his kindness and love.

I want to thank Ken Atchity and the folks at Story Merchant for all their help and guidance, Danny Donahue for his great illustrations, and Allison Warren for her tireless work on the audio book.

Last but not least I want to thank my father and mother for allowing me my own dreams, then showing me a way to make them come true. They are truly loved and dearly missed.

I was a boy, lamenting the discovery that Joe Barone was right, Santa Claus was a myth, when my mother sat me down by the Christmas tree and told me this story. Over the years I was able to learn more about her life as a coalminer's daughter.

I am proud to share her story on these pages.

Rowdy Herrington

GLOSSARY OF MINING TOWN TERMS

ALL... the word is used for something that is all gone... as in "the coffee is all."

BROGUE... A Heavy ankle high work boot.

CLUME... The mountain of waste taken from the mine.

COKE OVEN... An large oven used to bake coal, burning off the impurities and turning it into COKE to be used in the production of steel.

DINKY... A knitted cap.

DRUMMY... The hollow sound in the roof of a mine that indicates the danger of a cave in.

FLIP FLOP... The return trip with empty mine cars.

THE ELECTRIC... A Street car that runs on electricity.

GANDY DANCER... A worker who laid and maintained railroad tracks.

GAS... All talk and no substance.

GOB... Drainage ditch along a tunnel floor.

GROWLER... A miner's lunch bucket.

GUSH... A flood of water into the mine.

HAIR BOB... A ladies' hairstyle--cut and permed.

HALF HOLIDAY... A workday that ends at lunch.

IN DUTCH... To get in trouble

ON TICK... On credit.

PIT HELMET... A miner's hard hat.

PRIVY... An outhouse.

SHANTY... A small shack.

SLATE/SHALE... The waste rock take out of the mine with the coal.

SLATE WHEELER... A mine car used to carry the waste from the mine to the clume, where it is dumped

TIPPLE... Barn like structure where mining cars filled with coal are tipped upside down to empty them.

ABOUT THE AUTHOR

Rowdy Herrington is a screenwriter and feature film director. He lives with his wife Toni Semple on their ranch in Livingston, Montana, with two dogs, two cats, and four horses. This is his first novel.

A NOTE TO THE READERS

Please go to my Website, amazon.com, or the book forum of your choice, and post a review of FATHER CHRISTMAS. On my website you will find more information about the book and about me.

Thank you, Rowdy

www.rowdyherrington.com

CPSIA information can be obtained
at www.ICGtesting.com
Printed in the USA
LVHW111317181120
672034LV00026B/172